The
ALSFORD
Tradition

The
ALSFORD
Tradition

A Century of Quality Timber
1882–1982

by Patrick Beaver

HENRY MELLAND · London

First published in Great Britain
by Henry Melland Limited
23 Ridgmount Street, London WC1E 7AH

March 1982
Second edition April 1982

for J. Alsford Limited
Twickenham Road, Hanworth
Feltham, Middlesex TW13 6JJ

Designed by Norman Reynolds

ISBN 0 907929 00 1

Set in 11/13 point Photina Medium
Printed in England by Balding + Mansell,
London and Wisbech

Contents

BY THE SAME AUTHOR

The Big Ship
The Crystal Palace
A History of Lighthouses
A History of Tunnels
The Wipers Times
Victorian Parlour Games for Today
The Spice of Life
Yes! We Have Some (The History of Fyffes)
I.N.I.T.I.A.L. (The Story of the Initial Group)
All About the Home (The Story of Addis Limited)
A Pedlar's Legacy (The Origins and History of Empire Stores)
Sunderland Marine (The First 100 years)

Acknowledgments

The author wishes to thank all those of J. Alsford Limited and the Alsford family who have given him so much help in compiling this history. In particular, he is grateful to Mr Arthur Alsford for his painstaking research into his family history. Special thanks are also due to the company secretary, Alfred Smith, for his untiring and willing help.

It's unwise to pay too much, but it's unwise to pay too little. When you pay too much you lose a little money, that is all. When you pay too little, you sometimes lose everything, because the thing you bought was incapable of doing the thing you bought it to do. The common law of business balance prohibits paying a little and getting a lot. It can't be done. If you deal with the lowest bidder, it's well to add something to the risk you run, and if you do that, you will have enough to pay for something better.

JOHN RUSKIN (1819–1900)

Men seldom plant trees till they begin to be wise, that is till they grow old and find by experience the prudence and necessity of it.

JOHN EVELYN (1620–1706)

'Many a tree is found in the wood,
And every tree for its use is good.'

JOHN WEBSTER (1580–1625).

Evergreen Oak   Larch   Beech   Yellow Pine

Foreword

by Norman Welch

IT IS A PRIVILEGE to be invited to write a foreword to this absorbing history of the first hundred years of the Alsford timber business. Certainly it is a worthy addition to the select number of published histories of firms engaged in the timber trade of the United Kingdom.

In the last two decades there have been far-reaching changes in the structure and in the practice and methods of timber trading, while there has been, sadly for many, a sharp contraction in the number of companies and firms engaged in it through mergers and takeovers.

During this, for some, traumatic period Alsfords have prospered and extended their field of operations. Not only have they survived with increasing strength the testing years of transition, but today they rank among the most successful private companies in the trade by any criterion and their experience has led them to fear no challenge which the future can offer.

In the space of one hundred years (1882–1982) four generations of the Alsford family – all men of character, vision and business acumen with a capacity to evaluate economic and industrial trends – have created from humble origins an enterprise of diverse ramifications with imposing headquarters at Feltham, Middlesex, today embracing timber importing, merchanting and retailing with woodworking, forestry, home timber production, sawmilling and wharfinging.

The Alsford tradition clearly demonstrates the best features of the

9

private enterprise system of Britain and all the virtues associated with a sound family business of caring – about its customers, about its standards and reputation, about the quality of the goods it markets, about its employees – and jealous that its service shall be without peer among its competitors.

There have been a number of noteworthy achievements by the company over the years to which Patrick Beaver does full justice in his engaging recital of the Alsford saga especially by the move in the early days from London to the burgeoning suburb of Twickenham intriguingly foreshadowing the shape of things to come.

Despite his commitment to the exacting demands of a vigorous company employing a workforce of 260 and with 16 branches in the south-east of England, the present chairman and managing director, W. John Alsford, has found time to give unstinting service in the wider corporate sphere of the trade in which he is highly respected. He is a staunch and energetic supporter of the Timber Trades Benevolent Society of which he is a past national president and currently serves on the board of management. He has also been prominent in the affairs of the British Timber Merchants Association of which, too, he is a past president.

All who have enjoyed the pleasure of being associated with him in any activity or project (as the writer of this foreword can claim) cannot fail to be impressed by his shrewdness, dynamism, his sincerity and his warm-heartedness. He is the embodiment of all the qualities which have contributed to the company's progress and success and a true custodian of the Alsford tradition.

Norman Welch

Editor, Timber Trades Journal, 1949–77

INTRODUCTION
Touch Wood

Wood was the first material used by man for his own convenience and comfort: when he dwelt in caves it provided him with fuel, weapons and tools. Then, when he emerged, he used it to build his huts and boats for fishing and crossing water. Wood was essential to the development of civilisation and remains indispensable today.

Of the 30,000 and more species of wood-producing plants growing in the world, man uses only $1\frac{1}{2}$ per cent. These can be simply divided into two groups – hardwoods and softwoods – and a short definition of these terms is relevant to this history. From the point of view of the non-technical reader, it may be said that hardwoods are hard and softwoods are soft, although there are a few exceptions to this rule – balsa, for instance, is a hardwood. However, in Europe (but not in the tropics) hardwoods are deciduous – that is, they shed their leaves in winter – while softwoods, with the exception of the larch, are evergreens. The arboriculturist may add that hardwoods belong to the broad-leaved family and softwoods bear needle-leaves. But, apart from the odd exception, it can be again said that hardwoods are hard and softwoods are soft, both to work and feel.

Despite the replacement of wood in many fields by metals and plastics, the demand for it is greater today than ever before and the timber industry is among the biggest and most important in the world. Its structure is complex, but in simple terms it may be compared to the tree itself. The producers of wood are the roots from

which the whole edifice springs; the shippers, agents and importers
are the trunk through which the sap – otherwise the streams of sawn
timber – flows continually to the branches or outlets, and from them
to the twigs which are like the hundreds of industries and millions of
private users who depend upon wood to supply their various needs.

The firm of J. Alsford Limited, which is the subject of this history, is
unusual in that it performs all the functions of the industry referred
to above. It produces the whole of its home-grown timber
requirements from its own and surrounding woodlands, imports
large quantities of sawn wood from Russia, Finland, Sweden, the
USA and Canada and sells direct to the building industry and the
public through its many branches in south east England. And the
firm is unusual in another respect, for it is one of the oldest timber
merchants in the country, having been first established in the year
1882. Since then it has lived through six reigns and survived three
major wars as well as any number of economic crises. Yet,
throughout that hundred years, it has never ceased to grow. This is
remarkable because the timber trade relies mainly on the building
industry which is over-prone to economic recession and when
building firms go to the wall, their suppliers are liable to follow them.

There are a number of reasons that explain how the company has
survived and thrived over the years, but the key to its success may be
expressed in one word – 'tenacity' – a characteristic that is most
apparent in its insistence on dealing only with the best of materials.
Evidence of this tenacity runs through the company's entire history.
In searching world-wide for timber and in the seasoning, grading
and shaping of it for its various uses, the highest standards of quality
are maintained – quality upon which Alsfords' customers have
learned to rely. In the company's yards, every piece of timber is
individually examined and graded when it is imported; it is graded
again before being milled; before and after cutting and yet again
before being put into stock. The customer at Alsfords, be he home-
handyman or professional builder, is willing to pay that little more
for his timber because he knows that it is cheaper in the long run, for
he will find no excessively large knots, nor wain or other faults such
as poor shape and therefore he will have less waste.

It is a fact that the speed of growth of a tree depends directly upon
the climate at its location: the colder the climate the slower it will
grow; and the slower the growth the better will be the quality of the
wood. The geographical origin of any given shipment of timber is

recorded on the wood itself by the shippers mark and it is as a result of long and thorough experience of these marks, and thus of the shippers, that Alsfords' obtain timber with absolute confidence regarding its quality. There are thousands of timber shippers throughout the world but the company deals only with those who rank among the very best. In Finland these include those whose marks are KEMI, FENNIA⋈, ULEA and RA ⋈ HE and, in Sweden, ⋈ ROYAL ⋈. Timber bearing some of these marks comes from the arctic regions of Europe, and is of especial excellence.

The story of Alsfords and its traditional ways of working is the story of a family that has rigidly maintained its own code of excellence in materials and workmanship during an age when standards have tended to deteriorate: it is also the story of a firm that has proved itself capable of facing and adapting to the drastic social, economic and industrial changes that have been a feature of the twentieth century. The company's success can be aptly summed up in the words of the poet Oliver Wendell Holmes, who said: 'Knowledge and timber should not be used until they are seasoned.' The knowledge of Alsfords' craftsmen is, indeed, as well seasoned as the wood they handle. 'Touch wood' goes the saying and, as this story will tell, it is that special touch with wood, handed down through four generations, that is the open secret of the firm's success.

The business of the present company started in a small timber yard in Leyton in 1882, but its first discernible origins lie in a humble yard in Whitechapel in the early part of the 19th century.

PART 1

The Start of
a Business

THE NAME OF Alsford has been connected with timber for over 150 years, for in addition to the four generations who have successively built up the company that now bears their name, there were at least two earlier generations who worked with wood. One of these was James Alsford, the son of a cabinet maker, who was born in London in 1808 and who variously described himself as a mahogany dealer and an upholsterer. It is possible that he was a maker of furniture but it is certain that as a mahogany dealer he would have frequented Garraway's Coffee House in the City where mahogany was auctioned 'by the candle' which meant that bidding went on until a candle burnt down to a certain mark.

In 1840 James Alsford was living at 23 Upper Grove Street, Whitechapel and in that year he married Caroline Maw, a 28-year-old woman from Hertford. The ceremony took place at the Scion Chapel in Stepney and was conducted according to the rites of the 'Countess of Huntingdon's Society'. Over the following 20 years, Caroline bore James eight children – James, born in 1841; William, 1844; Caroline, 1848; Alfred, 1850; Rosetta Martha, 1852; Louisa, 1854; Mary Ann, 1858 and Benjamin, 1860. It was James, the eldest of these children, who laid the origins of the company that is the subject of this history and he will be referred to as James (1).

Little is known of the first 30 years of the life of James (1) except

James Alsford, the founder

Garraways Coffee House, Change Alley in the City c1873
Watercolour by Fred Shepherd
GUILDHALL LIBRARY, CITY OF LONDON

that he followed the trade of a plasterer and lath-maker. No doubt it was through the craft of lath-making that he gained his skill in grading wood, for good laths have to be made of wood that is free of faults.

James (1) was an adventurous and ambitious man and at the age of 30 he left England and his sweetheart, Harriet Bourne, to emigrate to Canada in search of his fortune. He was to be disillusioned, for he could obtain no work in which he could use his skills but was forced into a series of jobs ranging from shoe-cleaning to labouring on the building of the Canadian Pacific Railroad. In the last employment he suffered a rough existence, witnessed much brutality among his fellow workers and decided to return to England to set up his own business with the little money he had saved.

Arriving home in 1874 he married Harriet, rented a piece of waste land in Hornsey, and started a firewood business. In those days of coal fires, the firewood trade was an important one with hundreds of small 'firewood factories' operating in London. These were usually family affairs with the husband sawing and his wife splitting the wood into convenient sizes. This is probably how the two Alsfords worked in the early days. Most of the wood was sold to coster-mongers who, in turn, sold either direct to the public or to the small oil-shops in the poorer streets of London. The wood generally pro-cessed by the 'firewood factories' was not, as one would think, scrap or waste but for the most part consisted of light yellow deals imported from Sweden especially for the purpose. But James Alsford had another source of wood for his small business. He purchased wastage and spilt wood from the Surrey Commercial Docks, then the principal port for Britain's timber imports. In doing this he laid the foundations of the business now known as J. Alsford Limited.

The Beginning of Grading

When timber was being unloaded at the Surrey docks it was a regular occurrence for the slings of cranes to break so that pieces of wood fell into the water; also, when badly stowed, pieces frequently fell overboard from the barges on the way to their destination. This was especially liable to happen whilst the barges were negotiating locks. Because unloading was always given priority, this timber was left in the water but, from time to time, the Port of London Authority arranged to have the pieces gathered together and landed because they hindered the movement of shipping. This salvage was then made up into lots and sold at extremely favourable rates. Also included in these sales were quantities of dunnage – that is, pieces of timber stowed among a ship's cargo to keep it from injury by chaffing or wet. But whatever the source, this cheap dock timber usually contained a quantity of sound, good-quality material that only needed to be dried to enhance its value considerably. James (1) purchased large quantities of this material for conversion into firewood but in time, being a good judge of wood and a shrewd businessman, he realised that by spending a little time on selecting and drying out the best pieces in each parcel, he could sell them as

OVERLEAF
Greenland Dock, London c1881
by Tatton Mather
PAINTING FROM THE PORT OF LONDON AUTHORITY COLLECTION

good timber in competition with other merchants and by so doing he made a far greater profit than he could have earned by selling the entire lot as firewood. From there it was but a short step to give up the firewood trade and to become a timber merchant proper by purchasing parcels of timber at the fortnightly auctions that were then held at Winchester House in the City's Broad Street. The timber sold at these auctions was not in the form of entire cargoes but in small lots, usually of five standards,* being surplus of bills of lading from cargoes of shippers and importers not sold ex-ship.

Thus these sales were a safety valve of the trade and also the only source of small quantities of good timber available to merchants at low cost, for all lots were sold without reserve and often went for less than the cost of bringing the wood in.

James (1) was a strong and agile man as well he needed to be, for great endurance was required to buy on these occasions. The various parcels had to be inspected for quality and condition – a task that involved many hours of walking in the docks and the climbing of perhaps scores of stacks of wood. The auctions themselves took a whole day with a break at noon during which the bidders dined together at a local hotel. In this way the sales brought together many merchants, builders and contractors who would otherwise not have met and thus were of great benefit to all concerned. All in all, the auctions were the life blood of many small timber merchants each selling maybe only two standards of wood a week. They crowded the sale room – they lived by it. The terms were strictly cash and all timber had to be taken, '. . . as it lies at the Measurement raised on it . . . without any allowance for Faults or Defects, and to be cleared away within twenty days from the time of the sale, at the buyers expense'.

By using the skill he had acquired in his dunnage dealing, James was able to profit from parcels of timber that other merchants did not want. These were often odd sizes or goods that had partially deteriorated and were available for very low prices compared with the good parcels which were always at a premium. He could have immediately resold the wood and made a small profit but instead, through hard work, he graded it, converted it by hand to standard sizes and sold considerable quantities as construction and better class timber.

*The Petrograd standard was the timber measurement until metrication in 1971. It consisted of 165 cubic feet.

A New Start

It was while James was thus trading at Hornsey that an event occurred that was to have important effects on the company as it is today. The small plot of land on which he was trading was owned by the London, Midland and Scottish Railway Company, which, needing the ground for their own purposes, gave him seven days notice to quit. In the event, they evicted the up-and-coming timber merchant and moved his goods on to the street. James found temporary storage space for his now considerable stock of wood and looked around for a suitable site which he could buy freehold, for he had resolved never again to rent property for his business – a policy which, whenever possible, is followed by Alsfords today. A suitable site was eventually found at Gardners Corner in Wood Green and with the deeds to it safely in his possession, James moved his stock and recommenced his business. At Wood Green he engaged a small staff and installed his first sawmill.* Until then, the converting of timber into standard sizes, the cutting out of faults etc, had been done entirely by hand and this had severely limited the quantity of material the firm could handle. With his small, steam-operated circular-saw, James was able to increase his stock both in variety and quantity and his trade steadily increased. Much of this increase was due to an ever-growing reputation for good quality, for James, having graded his timber, took steps to preserve its condition. In his day a small timber yard was no more than a plot of land with maybe a ramshackle shed or two and the timber dumped anywhere – usually out in the wet. As new parcels of wood came in they were placed on top of existing stocks, leaving the older material to succumb to that old enemy of wood 'Merulius Lacrymans' or 'dry rot'. But James Alsford, with his feeling for wood, kept his material carefully stacked, covered and cared for and, above all, away from the wet. His timber was turned over in rotation, the practice being first in, first out. Thus he established another Alsford tradition.

It was at Wood Green that the firm started manufacturing and this mainly to keep the men and machines occupied during slack periods. Fencing, laths and battens were made at first and a good trade was built up in the making of folding trellis – which James Alsford claimed to have invented. Trellis manufacture came about almost

*History has failed to record the name of the man who made the first saw, although he ranks in importance with all other anonymous benefactors of the human race.

accidentally through a mistake James made at an early timber auction. At the sales run by Churchill & Sim at Winchester House it frequently happened that lots of similar size and quantity were offered in sequence, and the purchaser of the first lot was entitled to take the following lots at the same price unless there was a higher intervening bid. At an auction which James (1) attended when he was still inexperienced in the technique of bidding, a series of parcels of builders' laths were offered and James found that having taken the first lot and inadvertently nodding his head as the following were offered, he had acquired far more laths than he could possibly use; but, necessity being the mother of invention, he found a simple way of using the surplus by making extending diamond trellis. Through advertising this in the gardening journals he built up a steady connection which was invaluable in the early days. Trellis making by hand was continued by his son and grandsons up until 1924.

By 1877, the one-time lath-maker who had returned disillusioned from Canada only three years previously was the owner of a busy, prosperous, mechanised timber business with an ever-increasing custom. James Alsford decided that it was time to expand.

Early Growth

In those days it was an easy and simple matter to start a timber yard providing one had the capital to buy the initial stock. No local authority planning permission was required and there was little in the way of official regulations regarding facilities, fire-prevention, etc. If a man could occupy a piece of land and buy some timber he was in business. James Alsford did this a second time in about 1877 when he purchased a plot in Railway Approach, Edmonton and stocked it with wood he had accumulated at Wood Green.

Although by then he had two thriving yards, James continued with his policy of living frugally and returning his profits to the business. Thus, whenever sufficient money had accumulated, he purchased the freehold of another piece of land and opened another branch. In 1882, he bought two small adjoining plots in Lea Bridge Road, Leyton for £160 and there started the branch that is the direct ancestor of the present company. By 1891 there were Alsford yards at Wood Green, Hornsey, Harringay, Edmonton, Enfield and Leyton, all of which had been established within the space of 17 years.

James Alsford (2)

James Alsford (2)

Whilst building up his business, James Alsford still found time to raise a family of three children. The eldest was James (2), born in 1878, and there were two daughters, Harriet and Louisa. When old enough James (2) attended a local school for which his father paid 3d (1½p) a week and, as he grew up, he spent much of his spare and holiday time in training in all aspects of the timber trade under the tutorship of his father. Thus, he became familiar with the workings and atmosphere of the Wood Green timber yard. Often on Saturdays he helped the timber porters to ease their loads from cart to shoulder-pads. He had also been taken by his father to the Winchester House auctions where he learned a lot, not only about the physical nature of timber, but the subtle art of buying it. Then, at the Surrey Commercial Docks, he had often sat and watched timber being loaded from the decks of ships to barges alongside, then brought to the quay to be loaded as quickly as possible (to avoid demurrage charges) on to horse-drawn carts. And often he had sat on the top of a groaning timber-laden wagon to make the slow plodding journey

23

from Canning Town to Wood Green.* At the age of 14, James started full-time work at the yard and there he was treated like any other yard-boy; for there were no boss's son privileges for him. But he did learn about wood so that by the time he was 20 he knew as much about the subject as his father.

One of his first jobs was the firing and stoking of the boiler of the steam-engine which drove the mill machinery. Later he was put to sawing and planing at which he attained great skill. It should be explained that at the time there were few large planing mills in Britain and planed boards, floorings, skirtings, window boards and mouldings were imported from Sweden in considerable quantities. Much of this was to satisfy the demands of the building industry and of house building in particular for it was a time when the wealthy business and professional classes were seeking country and coastal properties. This market demanded only the very best of timber and, to supply it, James (1) purchased surplus lots of these goods, (especially mouldings) at the timber auctions and James (2) had the job of converting the pieces to smaller sizes. This very profitable operation was carried out through very fine sawing techniques which made it difficult to detect the sawn from the planed surface.

An Accident

Shortly after James (2) started work at Wood Green, there occurred a serious accident at the yard. While working at the circular-saw, the elder James was spoken to by a customer and, in turning to reply, his right hand became caught up in the saw and was severed. James was an extraordinarily cool man and after having a makeshift tourniquet applied to his arm, he held the severed hand in its place while being driven to the nearest hospital. Nothing could be done to save it.

But James Alsford did not allow this disability to interfere with his work, and shortly after the accident he built a cinema on the Wood Green site with storage space below it for his timber. Rented out to a film company, this was Wood Green's first cinema and for many years its only one. James continued to take an active and

*It is some indication of the possible perils of such a relatively short journey in those telephoneless days of horse-drawn transport, that in periods of snow and ice it was not unusual for timber-carters to take with them carrier-pigeons so that, in the event of the collapse or overturning of horse and/or cart, help could be summoned from the home-base.

enterprising part in running the timber business until his retirement in 1908.

It was intended by James (1) that his only son would, in time, take over the business but in 1898 a quarrel arose between them with the result that the younger James, always a rather sensitive individual, told his father to 'keep his yards' and walked out. The two men were never fully reconciled but James (1) eventually relented and started his son in business by giving him the Leyton yard and £10 in cash. With these assets, together with the small amount of money he had saved, James put his own name up at Leyton and in doing so he started the company as it is today.

Starting at Leyton

In leaving his father to start business on his own account, the younger James took with him more than a timber yard for, he had learned all his father's skills as a judge of and worker in wood; he had also acquired the principle of dealing only in the best quality goods and thus turned that principle into a tradition. Consequently his firm prospered from the start. In 1899 James married Mary Ann Elizabeth ('Lizzie') Cullingworth, the 19-year-old daughter of a Shoreditch upholsterer and they set up home in Walthamstow. By then the rift between the father and son was at least partially healed for James (1) attended the ceremony and acted as witness.

Looking west across the Baker's Arms junction at Leyton c1901. Alsfords' yard was on the open ground to the left
VESTRY HOUSE MUSEUM PHOTOGRAPHIC COLLECTION

Baker's Arms junction on the Lea Bridge Road c1905. Alsfords' yard was just beyond the London and Provincial Bank on the extreme right

Over the following years the Leyton business slowly expanded. Eventually James kept a staff of three helpers but, like his father, he did not cease to do his share of hard manual work, sawing, stacking, loading and unloading wood. There was no lifting tackle and no shelter from the weather and the hours were long. Work began at 6.00 am and continued until 8.00 am when half-an-hour was taken for breakfast. Then, at 8.30, the yard was opened for business and work continued until 5.30 pm. On returning home for his breakfast James would often say to his wife; 'I've had a good morning's work, so I'll stay at home today and have a rest.' Then, invariably, he returned to the yard to work throughout the afternoon.

James (2) continued the practice of buying odd parcels of wood by auction and to the skills he had learned from his father he added one of his own. This was an ability to judge how various standard-size pieces of wood could be cut from oversized thicknesses whilst, where possible, avoiding faults both natural and otherwise. Before bidding for any particular parcel he would carefully measure it. 'Ah! That's an eighth of an inch thicker than listed. I can use that eighth and make an extra 10 per cent.' If, for example, he found that pieces in a parcel of $1'' \times 4''$ were, in fact, $1\frac{1}{8}'' \times 4''$, he knew that even allowing for a saw-cut he could produce $\frac{5}{8}''$ and $\frac{1}{2}''$ pieces. But to do this successfully, considerable skill was required in setting up the saws, as the swage and shape of the teeth had to be set perfectly. This is where James' (2) earlier acquired skill was a great asset to the business and it was the development and passing on of that skill in setting wood-working machinery that was one of the keys to the firm's growth over the years and, indeed, it is an important element in the success of the company today.

In March 1912 James (1) died at the age of 71 whilst on holiday at Bournemouth, having retired from business four years earlier. The elder James had been a strong, shrewd man of business with a reputation in the trade for scrupulous fairness. Having given the Leyton yard to his son, so he had given his Manor Park branch to his daughter Louisa on her marriage to John Alcoe, a saw-miller who worked for Maples, the London furniture makers. The Alcoes did well at Manor Park and went on to establish an extensive business dealing mainly in hardwoods. Eventually they owned yards at Romford, Barkingside and Upminster. On the marriage of his second daughter, Harriet, James (1) presented her with his yard at Finchley.

After his business, James' greatest enthusiasm was for motoring – a sport he took up shortly after losing his hand, having had a special car built to allow for his disability. The number plate of that car, H 2729, is used today by his great grandson, John Alsford, the company's present chairman.

The Move to Twickenham

During the first 11 years of their marriage James and Lizzie Alsford had five children – James (3), born on 14th March 1901: William, 15th July 1903: Arthur, 12th December 1905: Winifred, 7th January 1908 and May Victoria who arrived on 25th May 1910. James (2) was fond of the countryside and detested London; often he was heard to declare 'I'm not bringing my family up in Walthamstow'. But it was not until 1914 that an opportunity arose for him to change his surroundings.

As a country lover James (2) joined a cycling club where he made many friends. One was Thomas Ellis, a builder, who married Lizzie Alsford's sister, Millie, and later opened his own timber yard at Uxbridge Road, Hanwell. James also made friends with David Rimmel, the owner of a timber yard at 52 Heath Road, Twickenham. Rimmel decided to emigrate in 1913 and put both his home and business up for sale. At that time Twickenham was a rapidly growing residential district and yet Rimmel's nearest competitors were no nearer than Richmond and Kingston. There was no doubt in James'

The first James Alsford's Lloyd and Plaister car c1901

W. John Alsford, the present chairman, and his car with the same
registration number

King Street, Twickenham c1900
LONDON BOROUGH OF RICHMOND UPON THAMES: LIBRARIES DEPARTMENT

mind that if he could succeed in the poor district of Leyton in competition with many others, then he could not fail in the fast-growing middle class town of Twickenham.

James at once started negotiations for the purchase of Rimmel's yard but, in the event, various obstacles and difficulties presented themselves. Fortunately, he was befriended by a local solicitor, James Montague Haslip*, through whose help, after nearly a year of protracted negotiations, James Alsford finally secured the business outright for £150.

There was a great deal to do before James (2) could realise his ambition of moving his family out of London. The yard, which was badly run down, had to be reorganised and properly stocked with materials that were up to the Alsford standard and a suitable house had to be found. Therefore he left the family at Walthamstow and spent most of his time at Twickenham, lodging at the home of William Fuller who was employed at Rimmel's yard and whose brother, Harry, was manager of the Leyton business. Eventually James bought a house in Popes Grove, Twickenham and moved into it with his family. Older members of the present Alsford family can

*Haslip was a member of the firm, Wilkinson, Kimbers & Staddon who are Alsfords' solicitors to this day.

1 James Alsford (3)
2 W.A. (Bill) Alsford
3 M. A. Elizabeth Alsford, *nee* Cullingworth,
  wife of James (2)
4 May Alsford, sister of Jim, Bill and Arthur
5 Mrs Maisie Cullingworth, mother of Mary Alsford
6 Child of Harriet Alsford
7 Eldest daughter of Harriet Alsford
8 Arthur Alsford, brother of Jim and Bill
9 James Alsford (2)

10 James Alsford (1)
11 Mrs James (1) Alsford
12 Harriet Alsford, daughter of James (1)
13 Louise Alcoe *nee* Alsford, wife of Jack Alcoe
14 Edward Alcoe
15 Daughter of Harriet
16 John Alcoe, son of Louise
17 Daughter of Harriet
18 Winifred Alsford, daughter of James (2)
19 Son of Harriet

Heath Road, Twickenham c1911. Shops are decorated for the Coronation of King George V

still remember the excitement of the train journey from grimy Walthamstow to their new home in the country – the walk from Twickenham station through the then quiet town, along Cross Deep, past the fine mansions bordering the Thames and their arrival at the house. For the children, now aged between 4 and 13, the change was magical, for they were within easy reach of the river and the open countryside and everything surrounding their new home was clean and new in contrast with the griminess of London. In addition there were within walking distance or by tram, the Royal Park at Richmond, Bushey Park at Teddington, Hampton Court with its Home Park running down to the Thames and, of course, the unrivalled botanical gardens of Kew.

When James took possession of Rimmel's business it was no more than a tumbledown shed behind a nameboard but by the time the family arrived at Twickenham it was a well stocked timber yard with good sound sheds for storing timber under cover. These James had built with his own hands and later he added another for a sawmill. Before long the business was well-established and its reputation for quality and good service spread among the local builders: furthermore, it was the only yard for many miles around where the small builder could obtain everything in the way of timber that he might require – weather-board, mouldings, battens etc. James was able to supply another demand – that of planed mahogany boards for punt-building. Such was the need for these that a combined saw and planer was laid down and a regular supply of logs obtained from London.

James and Arthur Alsford c1911

WALTHAMSTOW URBAN DISTRICT COUNCIL.

EDUCATION COMMITTEE.

T. W. LIDDIARD,
Secretary.

SCHOLAR'S TRANSFER FORM.

_____ School.   Date *April 8th 1914*

Name and Address.	Age.	Class	Reason given for leaving.	No. of attendances during present Sc.-yr.	No. of absences during present Sc.-yr.	Date of last attendance.	General conduct.	General remarks.
Alsford, James	13	2	Removal from District	302	0	8/4/14	Excellent.	Promoted to St.6 after six months in Standard 5th
Alsford, William	10	6	"	302	0	8/4/14	Good	Promoted to St.4 after 6 months in Standard 3.
Alsford, Arthur	8	9	"	302	0	8/4/14	Excellent	Promoted at the end of 6 mths

Signed *Geo. E Brown*

Head Teacher.

Form 302.—1,000. 5.12.

World War 1

No sooner was the business running smoothly than, in August 1914, the Great War broke out. The full extent of this disaster was not at first appreciated: 'It will all be over by Christmas' was the general view. The Great War was different from the many that Britain had fought, since for the first time the conflict had a direct and serious effect on the country's way of life and its trade. Industries that depended upon imports were the first to suffer and the timber trade was one of these, being early subjected to strict government control. Timber prices rose rapidly and there began a chronic shortage of supplies. Yet despite the fact that under those difficult conditions the business required all his attention, James (2) joined the West Sussex Regiment in 1916 and left his wife and 14-year-old James (3) to manage the business. This was especially difficult for Lizzie, for by then she had six children to manage, Robert Frederick having been born shortly after the move to Twickenham.

Following his father's example James (2) had given his son a

James Alsford's (2) first attempt at accounts, sent to his father

thorough training in the timber business and had sent him to manage Leyton when Harry Fuller enlisted. Later the yard was closed for the duration of the war and James (3) returned to Twickenham, taking over the general management of the entire business, buying timber, keeping the accounts and attending to the day to day running of the yard.

His brother William also started in the business, at the age of 14, by going into the Twickenham yard in 1917 where he stayed for a period before being sent to assist Lizzie's sister Millie at Hanwell whose husband Thomas Ellis was in the forces. Later he was sent to help a friend of his father, a Thomas Parker at Palmers Green, and eventually returned to Twickenham to take full part in the management with James (3).

The period 1916–8 was lean and troublesome for the family, for trade was bad owing to the shortages of timber and its ever-rising price. To make ends meet, the house in Popes Grove was sold and the family moved into a small terraced house in Grove Avenue, off Heath Road. In the garden, chickens were kept and vegetables were grown. It was hard work for Lizzie Alsford to assist in the business while running a home but she received much help from the older children From this mutual dependence there grew a family unity which was to prove invaluable in the later building of the business.

When the war ended James (2) came back to Twickenham, his family and his firm. Within a short time of his return the government removed all controls on the timber industry with the result that there occurred an unprecedented demand for wood – most of which was to fill the demands of the building and retail trade. Before very long the business was thriving as never before and the Alsfords were able to move back to Popes Grove into a large house which stood exactly opposite their old one. For the family this was the start of a new era.

Building a Business

The post-war trading boom was short-lived and in 1921 a general slump had set in. The timber trade was particularly badly hit with the price of wood falling almost overnight from £40 a standard to £20, causing the ruin of many large merchants. The combined stock of the two Alsford yards was halved in value from £10,000 to £5,000 but James, always the realist, shrugged his shoulders, halved his prices and forgot the loss.

James Alsford (3), *Mr Jim*

Arthur Alsford followed his brothers into the firm in the spring of
1921 at the age of 16, his relatively late entry being due to his
attending the Acton and Chiswick Polytechnic, a day training school
run by the Middlesex Education Committee. Here he studied most
aspects of the building trade as well as other general subjects for a fee
of 10s 0d (50p) a term. The knowledge he gained was to prove
invaluable to the company during its later rapid development. Each
of the boys had to be willing to do every job connected with the
business no matter how humble. They did office work, loaded and
unloaded timber and, when required, delivered advertising circulars
from door to door. At the same time each received a thorough
training in the practical side of the business, learning not only the
skills of grading wood but those of working it. Over the next few years
the unique characteristics and interlocking abilities of the three
brothers began to emerge.

In 1921 a programme of expansion began with the purchase of
Nos 63/65 Heath Road, then an empty plot opposite the
Twickenham yard and by July 1922 permanent buildings for storage
had been erected on the site. Then, in September 1922 another

William Alfred Alsford, *Mr Bill*

Arthur Leonard Alsford, *Mr Arthur*

Receipt for Arthur Alsford's first motor-cycle, a Sunbeam purchased 1926

branch was opened in Station Yard, Mortlake, which Arthur was sent to manage. In the period 1922–4 sales expanded yearly and as the firm was without sufficient manufacturing capacity, James (3) took over the purchasing from his father and was soon buying whole bills of lading. In doing this he started the system of barging the timber from the ships in the London docks to wharves at Twickenham, Mortlake and Brentford where William, in complete control and with an enthusiasm which affected everyone, organised and took part in the unloading, transport and delivery of the timber to the yards direct. The work was done with seconded and part-time labour. The aim then was (as it is now) to have the timber unloaded and stowed under cover in the finest condition, each piece being stacked by hand with a regular space between to speed seasoning.

It was one of these occasions that eventually led James (3) to confine himself entirely to administration, for while inspecting and helping to unload the first consignment of mixed planed goods he received a serious injury which incapacitated him for a year.

In 1924 a Sagar 2 × 4 fourcutter and a circular-saw was installed in the rear building at 63/65 Heath Road and shortly afterwards the adjoining plot, Nos 67/69, was purchased and temporary timber sheds erected by William and his work team. The manufacture of mouldings, planed battens and small quarterings then started with Arthur in charge of the sales side. James (2) took an active part in running the mill, putting into practice all the skills and the knowledge he had acquired through his 32 years in the trade. When the mill was running smoothly James (2) invited his brother-in-law, Alfred Cullingworth, to join the company. Cullingworth was an expert machinist who became foreman of the sawmill and later the firm's saw doctor.

During this period, James (3) and William were active in searching for suitable sites for new branches and in 1926 a yard was started at St Marks Hill, Surbiton. William Tomkins, the firm's first lorry driver, was made manager of this branch and a little later, Fred Waite (the driver who succeeded him) became manager at Mortlake. These moves were in accord with the company's policy of promoting from within whenever possible – a policy which is followed today. During the year of the general strike of 1926 the fourth of the Alsford children, Winifred, entered the business as secretary and book-keeper and remained in that position until her marriage to Kenneth Howes in 1930. In 1927 the firm had four outlets which between them were producing a gross profit of nearly £10,000 – a consider-able margin for a small business in those days. But James (2) put the

An Alsford timber yard and delivery vehicle c1930

Alsfords' 1928 Price List showing the front cover and two of its 80 pages

Heath Road, Twickenham . . .

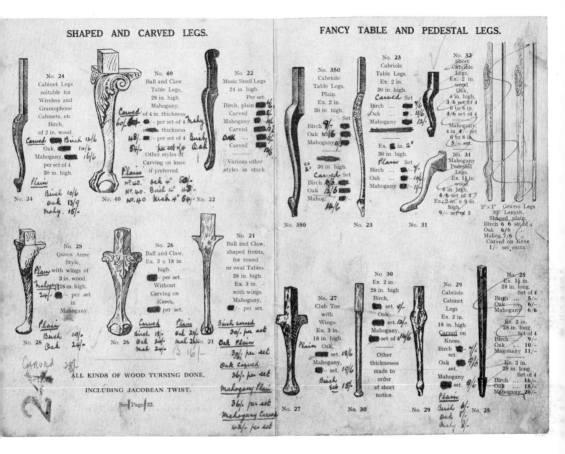

... and adjoining yard in the 1930s

major part of the nett profits back into the business, thus continuing the principle established by his father. In 1929, Robert, the youngest of the Alsford boys, started work in the Heath Road yard where he too gained a thorough knowledge of the trade.

In 1928 new offices and a garage were built at Surbiton and in the same year the original premises at Twickenham were converted into what was possibly Britain's first 'do-it-yourself' shop and store. Here were sold mouldings and a number of woods that were in local demand – ash for repairing carts, Japanese oak, a range of materials for furniture making and various woodworking accessories and sundries. Alsfords also made up and sold what were probably the first DIY kits, these being for the making of wireless-set cabinets and containing fretworked fronts, baffle boards and even a small square of silk for the loudspeaker. The store held a stock of 1,000 imported doors and gates, a large stock of Essex Board (the first wall-board to be manufactured) and a range of plywood in all sizes.

The 1930s

The year 1929 will long be remembered in British industry for then began the great slump of the 1930s. The effect of the depression on the timber trade was severe. Many merchants found themselves glutted with timber for which there were no buyers and in consequence prices fell steadily. One example was the average price of Swedish redwood battens which in 1930 was £13 10s 0d a standard; in 1931 it was £11 10s 0d; in 1932, £10 10s 0d and in 1933, £9 15s 0d. The slump in the timber trade came at the height of a continuing post-war building boom which was especially evident in the area in which Alsfords were trading. Much of this activity was termed 'jerry building' but it should be remembered that many of the so-called jerry built houses are as sound today as when new and this was because they were, for the most part, constructed with sound materials. Here the Alsford tradition paid off, for it was on the firm's reputation for consistently good quality and service that it continued to expand during this most difficult period.

To expand a timber business at a time when similar firms were going bankrupt by the dozen was no mean achievement, especially by a man like James (2) who would only buy freehold property and who did not hold with owing money – even to a bank. It meant hard

'Holmwood', Datchet, where James Alsford (2) spent
many happy years with his family

work and a modest standard of living to allow for the re-investing of all profits in new modern machinery, improvement of premises and the purchase of new yards. And, most important, there was his ever-insistent demand for quality. On one occasion an old customer pointed out to him a slight flaw he had found in a piece of timber he had purchased earlier. 'You're quite right,' said James after examining the wood, 'and that's not the sort of thing that we want to sell. You can have the whole load with my compliments if you like.'

In looking through an Alsford price list of the 1930s one can fully appreciate the extent of today's monetary inflation. Builders' ladders were on sale at 1s 0d (5p) a rung; laths were 3s 3d (17p) for a bundle of 500 feet; unplaned battens, 5 feet a penny ($\frac{1}{2}$p); chestnut fencing, 1s 7d (8p) a yard and rustic arches, 12s 6d (62$\frac{1}{2}$p) each. There were dolly-tubs,* coppersticks, clothes posts, aerial poles and, of course, trellis. Most of these items were made at the yard during slack periods. The shop also did a regular trade in turned bannister-posts, for in those sterner days poor families frequently burned their bannisters for warmth or even cooking and new ones were needed when an unfortunate family was eventually evicted.

*Dolly-tubs were wooden vessels for washing clothes with a 'dolly' – ie, a wooden appliance shaped like a doll used for agitating the clothes by hand.

PART 2

The Growth of a Business

JAMES (3) WAS, like his father, a man of some vision and he was determined to expand the firm not only in size but in scope. Part of his ambition was to import timber direct from the shippers and, in time, to acquire a wharf. As the person most concerned in buying the firm's timber, he had a close and regular contact with one Kenneth Miles, a representative of the timber agents, Gordon Watts & Company Limited. Miles had for some time considered going into the timber-importing business on his own account and often discussed the possibilities of this with James (3). James was thinking of starting a firm of importers at that time, for he calculated that he could buy whole consignments of timber direct from shippers, partly to satisfy Alsfords' requirements and sell the remainder and additional bills of lading elsewhere, thus ensuring the availability of regular supplies of the right materials at the right price without a middle man. Eventually the two men agreed on a practical proposition and, after discussions with the rest of the family, James concluded a partnership agreement with Miles as a result of which the company, Alsford & Miles Limited, was incorporated on 28th September 1932 to conduct business as a timber importer with offices at Bush House in London's Aldwych. The new firm started with a capital of £2,000 in

A forest in Finland, from where some of the company's timber is imported
OULU OSAKEYHTIO, TIMBER SALES

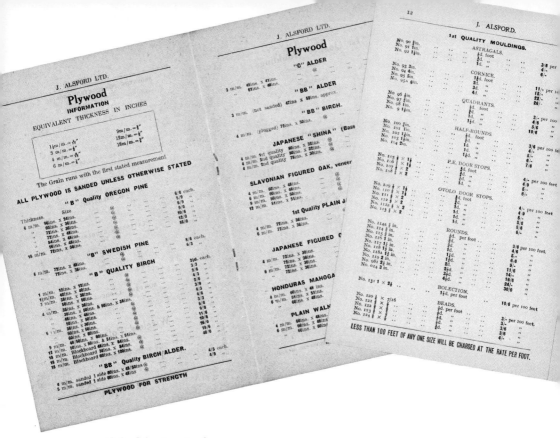

Alsfords' prices in the 1930s

shares held by James (2), James (3), William and Arthur Alsford and Kenneth Miles. James' (3) wife, Doris, was appointed secretary to the company and business was started. For its purpose, the capital was meagre and financing was mostly by bills receivable and payable – which meant that sales had to be in balance with purchases. For James (3) the running of the new company was a full-time job and this necessitated leaving the day to day running of Alsfords to his brothers. Shortly after the commencement of business, the firm was joined by W. R. J. (Bob) D'eath as a junior clerk, a loyal and stalwart employee who played an important part in the events which followed. May Alsford joined Alsford & Miles Limited as a book-keeper and when Doris resigned in 1934, she took over as secretary – a position she held until 1946.

Alsford & Miles Limited flourished from its beginning, for James (3) was a shrewd and experienced buyer of wood who always knew exactly what he wanted and where to get it. Miles worked on the selling side and continued in that capacity until he resigned from the

firm in 1935 to attend to other business interests. Thereafter Alsford & Miles Limited was entirely in Alsford hands.

In 1932 Alsfords opened a branch in Raynes Park and by 1933 with all the branches making good profits, James (2) went into semi-retirement leaving the management of the business in the hands of his four sons.

The creation of Alsford & Miles Limited meant in effect that the established firm of J. Alsford was in the fortunate position of being its own importer and the result of this arrangement was reflected in a steady increase in turnover from £28,000 in 1933 to £47,000 in 1939.

The Feltham Development

It will be remembered that the sister-in-law of James (2) married Thomas Ellis who started a timber yard at Hanwell. In 1936 Ellis decided to retire and, as a result of the family connection, the four Alsford brothers acquired the assets and business of the Hanwell yard. This further addition, together with the steadily increasing sales of the business as a whole, created a pressing need for more space at Twickenham which was then the supply depot for the various branches. It was therefore decided in January 1937 to buy a site on the outskirts of Twickenham as a reserve against the expected continuation of the firm's expansion and a $4\frac{1}{2}$ acre plot of land, then little more than a water-logged gravel pit, was found at Feltham, three miles from Twickenham. In buying this site, the Alsford brothers intended to convert part of it into a large covered timber store to house the timber purchases of Alsford & Miles Limited but it was also intended eventually to move into the home-grown timber trade and, with this in mind, detailed plans were produced for a sawmill and other machinery. As will be seen, this was a most fortuitous step. Work was at once started to drain and level part of the ground. With this accomplished, two sheds were built for the future storage of timber.

It so happened that in June 1938 there was a major road widening of Heath Road Twickenham with the consequent loss to the company of a quarter of their site and the loss of the frontage of the buildings. This came as a mixed blessing for although the company regretted the loss of yard space, the compensation received was sufficient to erect the buildings that stand today at 63/69 Heath Road. The design and planning of the buildings was entrusted to H.

Lea Bridge Road, Leyton c1930. Alsfords' yard was just beyond the sign RADIO on the right

VESTRY HOUSE MUSEUM PHOTOGRAPHIC COLLECTION

Langford Moyle, a local architect, and as a result of his skill in negotiating with the local planning authorities most of the company's requirements were incorporated in the final designs.

During late 1938 and early 1939 an important internal re-organisation concerning the ownership of the firm's properties took place, whereby the Alsford Land Investment Company was formed to purchase all the land and buildings owned by the Alsfords, with the exception of the Leyton yard which was owned personally by James (2).

In April of 1939 the decision was then made whereby Alsford & Miles Limited purchased certain assets of J. Alsford and thus effectively merged the two concerns as one. The name of the new organisation was changed to J. Alsford Limited. This move, in conjunction with the Feltham development, was to have the most important consequences in view of the war that broke out later that year.

World War 2

On Friday, 1st September 1939, 250 standards of timber consigned to J. Alsford Limited arrived at Twickenham wharf to await collection by the firm's lorries. As it was apparent that war would soon break out, it was a matter of urgency to get that timber 'off the water' and into the Feltham yard as soon as possible. There were two reasons for the urgency. First, that the load would be liable to requisition as long as it remained in the barges and second, because it was expected that the firm's lorries might also be commandeered when war was declared. To deal with the emergency, James (3) visited all the branches asking for volunteers to spend the weekend unloading the wood and moving it to Feltham. Each volunteer – from branch manager to yard-boy – was to receive £1 10s od (£1.50) for the two days work. The response was wholehearted and on the day preceding the outbreak of the war, the entire male staff began the considerable task of transferring the 550 tons of wood from barges to the firm's lorries. It was then taken to Feltham where it was stacked in the sheds. The work was supervised by James, William and Arthur Alsford who took off their coats and laboured with the rest. It was back-breaking work, especially for the office staff, but later all agreed that it was one of the most enjoyable weekends they could remember. A spirit of comradeship prevailed –

Arthur Weston and Les Saunders

Harry and Arthur Weston
Les Hayes with the 'Dennis Horla'

the same spirit that motivated the British people throughout the six years that followed. War was declared on the Sunday but the work continued throughout the day despite the sounding of the first air-raid warning. By Sunday evening all the wood was safely stored and under temporary cover at the Feltham yard.

The merging of the importing business with that of the retailing, together with the securing of this considerable quantity of timber had the most fortunate of effects for when, but a few days later, the supply of timber came under government control, Alsfords received a quota that was based not only on the retailing side of the business but also on the quantity of its imports. Consequently, the company was given a yearly allocation of wood that was far greater than would have been granted had the merger not taken place. Thus, throughout the difficult years that followed, the firm continued to operate successfully.

Another important event at about this time was that the Leyton branch was closed and the manager, Harry Fuller, retired. Thus was severed a link with the firm's origins that was established in 1882.

Following the outbreak of war there was a sudden large demand for timber for air-raid shelters and black-out frames but this did not compensate for a drastic fall in demand from the building trade which virtually came to a standstill. Consequently turnover dropped from £95,000 in 1939 to £60,000 in 1940. Another factor in this fall was the closing of the DIY shop in Heath Road, for it was evident that this trade could not survive in war-time. Then the manufacture of mouldings was discontinued although, as it happened, the firm's stock of mouldings lasted through the war years, mainly because people were more interested in repairing air-raid damage, boarding up windows and building air-raid shelters than they were in putting up fancy mouldings in their homes. Other early effects of the war were the closing of the planing plant through shortages of labour and materials and, as expected, the requisitioning of half the firm's lorries. Those that remained were formed into a pool that served all the branches. Later, they were supplemented by three powerful motorcycles fitted with extended side-cars.

The declaration of war found the government fully prepared to take over control of the timber industry and almost overnight a Timber Control Department was established by the Ministry of Supply to deal with the purchasing, shipping, importation and consumption of timber. Then, in 1940, came the occupation of

Charles Howells (centre) who helped Alsfords to build air-raid shelters, with Arthur and James Alsford

Norway with the subsequent control of the Baltic by Germany and, with the cutting off of all Baltic supplies, Britain turned to the USA and Canada. There can be no doubt that without Canadian timber many British industries would have collapsed. As supplies dwindled during 1940 so the demand for timber increased – especially for materials for repairing bombed buildings. Like all others in the trade, Alsfords had considerable difficulty in ensuring that their regular customers were supplied and very little was available to fill the ordinary customer's official ration of one pound's value of wood a month. War-time price-control posed yet another problem for, although still concerned with the quality of what it sold, the firm could ask no higher prices than those of its competitors. Nevertheless, the policy of grading for quality was continued.

One of the most lethal blows delivered to London by the German Air Force during the war was the bombing of the London docks on 7th September 1940. The huge timber storage yards of the Surrey Commercial Docks were set alight from end to end and the blaze continued for a week. After this disaster the government ordered that the nation's store of timber be dispersed as widely as possible with the result that timber depots were established around the perimeter of Greater London. One of these depots was Alsfords' yard at Feltham where, until the end of the war, every spare space was packed with part of the nation's reserve stock of wood.

During the war the company continued to develop. The timber

London Docks ablaze after the first air raid on 7th September 1940

yard and home-grown sawmill of T. H. Harte in Worthing was acquired in 1943 and, managed by Robert Alsford in the typical Alsford manner, continued Harte's production of sea-defence timbers, railway-sleepers and other timbers for the war effort. At Feltham, more building was undertaken and much electrification installed to replace the old steam-powered machinery. But the most important war-time development was the implementation of the firm's earlier decision to move into the home-grown timber trade.

Home-grown

For thousands of years before the recorded history of Britain, vast forests of oak covered much of England and Wales; then, from the Middle Ages onward, great areas of these forests were steadily felled.

Industry was the greatest consumer of this wood. Enormous quantities were used for the making of charcoal, smelting of iron and the making of glass while agriculture and house building also took a

Home Grown TIMBER

to

HELP THE WAR EFFORT

Sawn to Specification

Oak, Ash, Chestnut, Elm, Beech, Fir
for
SHIPS, RAILWAYS, MINES
and other Essential Industries

TELEGRAPH & TRANSMISSION POLES
DEALS, BATTENS, BOARDS, PRIME BUTTS

Your Enquiries are invited

J·ALSFORD
LIMITED

ENGLISH TIMBER MERCHANTS
Dept. W., Sawmills, Twickenham Road, Hanworth, Feltham, Middlesex

Telephone : Feltham 2264 (3 lines)

share. Then came the vast and unprecedented demand for oak to build the great fleets of warships which defended the shores of Britain and later built the Empire. All these demands were met by native hardwood but in the 19th century there occurred a change to a need for softwoods: this was due mainly to the rapid increase in population which created a demand for cheap houses. For such, the hardwoods, such as oak, elm and chestnut, were too heavy and hard to work; they were also expensive. The coal mines and the railways also demanded considerable quantities of softwoods – particularly for pit-props and sleepers. By the middle of the 19th century home resources were inadequate to satisfy these ever-increasing demands and imported timber dominated the market. By the 1930s the home-grown trade was supplying no more than 4 per cent of British consumption but in 1940, when the extent of the emergency became clear, it rose to the occasion splendidly. Stout old oaks, rugged elms and thousands of firs and pines that enhanced the British countryside were felled by the axe of the woodman. Thousands of Commonwealth lumberjacks, helped by Britain's 'lumberjills' – members of the Woman's Timber Corps – were employed on this work under the direction of the Home-grown Timber Department of the Ministry of Supply and as a result the output of native timber increased from 75,000 standards in 1939 to 297,000 in 1942.

With the ever dwindling supply of imported wood and the resurgence of the home-grown trade, the company decided immediately to implement its pre-war plans for a home-grown mill at Feltham and the necessary machines were installed there. The first tree processed was a large walnut bought standing in a backgarden in Twickenham. The next purchase was of several poplars growing in the grounds of Syon House. They were felled and floated down the Thames from Isleworth to Twickenham wharf.

It was during these early felling operations that William Alsford took full control of the newly-formed forestry section and exploited his undoubted business ability in dealing with owners and agents: finding, measuring and buying the standing timber, controlling the fellers and forestry workers and extracting the felled trees. All this was done with a thoroughness and enthusiasm that inspired confidence and respect. In this work he was helped by his brother Robert.

Advertisement from *Wood* March 1943

Following this apprenticeship to the home-grown timber trade the company purchased all the standing softwood timber on 250 acres at King's Ride, Ascot, which was ideal for conversion into pit-props and telegraph-poles. The trees were felled, trimmed and loaded on to tractor-drawn pole-wagons for despatch, the better logs being sent to Feltham for sawing. The entire area was cleared by six fellers in 12 months – a major achievement when it is considered that all the felling was accomplished by hand.

Many other felling projects followed and eventually the clearance was undertaken of 200 acres of mixed woodlands on the Lovelace Estate at Effingham. This was a selected felling operation carried out with chain-saws and it took two years to complete. Throughout these early felling operations a good trade in round timber sales was built up and, to handle it, the haulage fleet and sawmill grew steadily. By the time Effingham was cleared the Feltham mill was working two shifts and the firm was advertising itself as 'English Timber Merchants' offering 'Home-grown timber sawn to specification. Oak, ash, chestnut, elm, beech, fir for ships, railways, mines and other essential industries'.

When the firm made its first tentative steps into felling and hauling timber it had little experience of this trade. The men were unskilled in forestry as, indeed, was the management. Often the tractors hauling the logs bogged down in mud, until a change was made to caterpillar wheels. Later, the trimmed trees were winched up skids on to the pole-wagons by tractor. But at the completion of the Effingham operation, William Alsford had created a highly efficient forestry section which was capable of competing with any similar organisation in the country. Its chance to prove this came in 1946 when the company purchased the standing timber on a section of a 2,000 acre estate at Wadhurst, Sussex. To part-process the logs on site, a small sawmill was erected by William Alsford and Herbert (Bert) Edwards, a thoroughly experienced forester who had recently joined the company from the Forestry Commission. The sawmill was driven by a 42hp Ruston diesel-engine which powered two saw-benches, some smaller machines and lighting. Eight men were employed in the mill and, in gangs of three, others felled the trees. It was fortunate that there was nearby a large German POW camp and

Sawmill and log pond of Kemi Oy, Finland, one of Alsfords' suppliers

James Alsford (3) on extreme right . . .

the prisoners, otherwise idle, were available for work. They were employed by Alsfords in loading and a gang of six would fill a six-ton lorry for 10s 0d (50p) to share between them – and they were very pleased to get it.

Back to Normal

When the war ended in 1946, the company decided on a further programme of expansion to meet the anticipated post-war boom in the building industry. The first opportunity taken was the acquisition of the Eastbourne joinery firm of T. Beal & Company Limited, a firm specialising in good quality 'one-off' jobs, such as oak staircases for hotels, business premises, etc. Not being in Alsfords' line, this work was phased out and the factory converted to the manufacture of doors and window frames for sale in the branches; timber merchanting was also introduced.

In the following year James (3), with his flair for recognising an opportunity, encouraged his brothers to purchase from the Ministry of Supply the prefabricated steelwork of a large aircraft hanger which, with the skilled help of a Hampton firm of structural

Complimentary Dinner

TO

MR. I. J. O'HEA

GIVEN BY

THE U.K. TIMBER DELEGATION
TO BRITISH COLUMBIA

BALATON ROOM, HUNGARIA RESTAURANT
REGENT STREET, LONDON, S.W.1

TUESDAY 6TH DECEMBER 1949

. . . cover of menu

engineers, S. J. Cadwell Limited, was adapted to make two smaller buildings of 11,600 and 12,600 square feet respectively, both high enough to allow for the stacking of timber with fork-lift trucks. The sheds were erected at Hanworth on reinforced chequered concrete bases which were laid by an enthusiastic team of four Alsford men supervised by William and Arthur.

At the time the first building was completed, the government began releasing the national stocks of timber and sent lists to merchants which described the quantities and qualities available. Together with the manager of the Twickenham branch, Harry Osborne (who had joined the company in 1933), James embarked on a tour of inspection of the available timber with a view to putting in tenders. Buying from the national stock was a task that called for cool judgement, for the release of those large quantities of wood resulted in a speculative urge in the market which caused many anxious moments for buyers large and small. But, by acting promptly and using the traditional Alsford skill in selection, the company obtained a large quantity of fine Russian timber – a quantity that was limited only by the amount of finance available. After the shortages and rationing of the war years and the inferior quality of much that was available, it was a joy to both management and staff to see and handle this huge amount of beautiful golden yellow timber and all concerned remember that when the last load was safely under cover at Feltham they went home tired but happy and relaxed.

The acquisition of this timber was extremely helpful to Alsfords for it enabled the firm to keep going whilst re-establishing contacts with foreign shippers. Some goods were obtained through the timber auctions that were revived after the war, but this facility was short-lived; for a practice soon arose that is at variance with the very principles of sale by auction – namely, that if goods are sold without reserve, the seller must accept whatever price they fetch. But at the revived auctions some sellers were deputing persons to 'bid up' their goods and instructing brokers to 'protect' them up to a certain figure. The buyers, realising what was happening, took the obvious course of staying away and the auctions eventually stopped. Thus the attempt to revive softwood auctions failed and another of Alsfords' links with its origins was broken.

The buildings erected from the 'government surplus' materials proved ideal for Alsfords' purpose and as the early storage sheds at Feltham had become obsolete, Cadwells were commissioned to design and erect two more sheds. Thus Feltham was provided with undercover storage space for sawn and manufactured timber adequate for the forseeable future.

Other developments at Feltham at about this time included the building of kilns for drying English hardwood planks and, in 1947, a new planing and sawing mill together with sawdoctoring and cutter shops. James (3) was of great assistance in the equipping of the mill, saw and cutter shops, for he was an expert on machine tools who had been appointed as a member of the government's Machine Tool Control at the end of the war.

Later in 1947, James (3) was invited to join the Timber Trade Federation's delegation to Canada. This became one of the highlights of his life, for through it he made many friends among the larger importers. His Canadian trip resulted in two benefits for the company: the purchase of the first fork-lift truck and the subsequent supplies of magnificent timber from the Hillcrest Lumber Company of Vancouver Island.

At about that time an important and lucrative trade was started in supplying mouldings of the finest quality to the British film industry.

These mouldings, which were used in elaborate interior settings, had to be speedily made and delivered. The Riverside studios at Hammersmith were the first customers in this field and the reputation gained there for first-class work and service soon spread to other film companies and before long the studios at Twickenham, Pinewood, Shepperton and Ealing were being supplied with mouldings especially made to their individual designs.

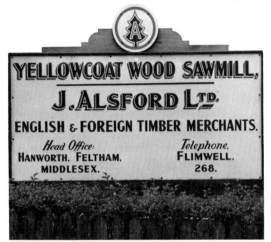

There is a legend that during the Baron's War in 1264, in the Parish of Ticehurst at a place then called 'Flemenewelle', a gathering of yellow-coated archers, loyal to Simon de Montfort, had 'sniped' at King Henry III's army as he marched to the Battle of Lewes. The enraged King ordered every archer wearing a yellowcoat to be beheaded, and they were butchered like so many lambs in a fold

Yellowcoat Wood

In 1949, home-grown timber was freed from government control and as a result there began another important chapter in Alsfords' history.

By the end of the war home-grown timber in Britain accounted for some three-quarters of domestic consumption. In the field of mining-timber it had entirely replaced imported material to the extent of several million tons a year. But despite this the home-grown industry declined rapidly when European imports reappeared. Many producers dropped out simply because they could not compete with imported timber which, because of the vast scale on which it is produced, can be shipped to this country at highly competitive rates:

H. J. (Bert) Edwards, manager of Wadhurst and later of Yellowcoat Wood

indeed, one of the difficulties faced by the home-grown timber market is that it costs practically as much to transport a load from Scotland to London as it does to bring a similar load in from Sweden. Nevertheless, Alsfords considered that with their special knowledge and experience of timber selection and grading they could remain in the home-grown trade at a profit. The decision to remain was made in 1949 as a result of an unexpected turn of events at Wadhurst where the firm was still engaged in felling and milling.

At the time when Alsfords were completing their second year's work at Wadhurst the estate was sold and the company was given one month's notice to quit the land and to remove their saw mill and the £50,000 worth of felled timber which lay there on the ground – far more than could be processed and moved to Feltham within the time given. A decision was therefore made to find a suitable area of woodland near Wadhurst, to transport both timber and machinery and to start up in the home-grown timber trade independently – for it will be remembered that up to that time the company owned no woodland and, in all its history, had never planted a tree.

A search was at once started for a suitable site and this was found by the manager of the Wadhurst works, Herbert Edwards, who had many years of experience in forestry and the timber industry. The site he chose comprised 36 acres of scrub woodland known as

Yellowcoat Wood which lay just off the Hastings Road, Flimwell, Sussex, five miles from Wadhurst. The site was purchased freehold for £1,500, the Wadhurst timber taken there and, after permission was obtained from the local council, the mill dismantled, taken to Flimwell and re-erected. Much had to be done before operations could begin on the new site. There was no drainage, no power and no road – only a narrow cart-track running through what was otherwise mud. William Alsford supervised the work while living in a caravan on the site. Rough wooden sheds were erected for the mill and for offices: a narrow-gauge railway built to bear hand-propelled carts; concrete beds constructed for the mill and its engine and, for cooling, a system of rain-water collection devised. With the mill installed and operating, work re-commenced on sawing the Wadhurst timber with locally recruited labour.

When purchased, the Flimwell site comprised half of good chestnut coppice and half of scrubland. The chestnut was kept and

Nine years of timber growth at Yellowcoat Wood, planted by Bill Alsford, Bert Edwards and their staff

developed into a fine wood while the scrub was planted with conifer. This first conifer wood is flourishing but still intact, for it takes up to 80 years for a conifer to mature. Tree growing is, indeed, a long-term project. Good oak, for example, may be 200 years old before it is ready for felling and it is possible that some of the oak being planted at Flimwell today may not be used until the middle of the 22nd century and, if this is so, it is interesting to speculate as to the use to which it will be put. And yet, this far-seeing policy makes sound economic sense for good standing timber is always available as a reserve that is appreciating in value at approximately three per cent per annum – and this is apart from inflation and enhanced value resulting from increased demand.

There is in some sections of the trade a view that all British timber is inferior in quality, but this is not so. The native softwoods, being faster growing trees, are indeed somewhat inferior in strength but they can be put to many uses and there is always a market for them. But British hardwoods – the oak, the ash and the beech – are all beautiful timbers much in demand by the furniture and cabinet making trades.

Since the Flimwell project began, cutting has only been undertaken as part of forestry management (that is, to improve the woods by thinning out what is already there to allow the main crop to reach maturity in its own time), so the timber yield from Yellowcoat Wood is nowhere near enough to supply the sawmill. To augment the supply and to keep the mill busy, standing timber is purchased over a radius of 30 miles; this includes trees from the Forestry Commission, farms and estates. After felling, trimming, preliminary grading and sawing, the timber is subjected to the strict scrutiny which ensures that every piece is put to its best use. The better hardwood logs are stored, cut into planks and air-dried for the eventual end-use of joinery and cabinet-making, whilst the lower quality hardwoods are cut to various sizes for the fencing trade. The softwoods are similarly graded, the better quality being cut to construction-size timber to supplement the shortage of imported softwood.

End of an Era

Soon after the company planted its first trees in Yellowcoat Wood there occurred, on 11th January 1951, the death of James (2) at the age of 73. He had retired from active participation in the business a few years previously although he remained as a director to contribute his long experience to the running of the firm. In the earlier days he knew all his employees by name and took an interest in them and their families and he grieved when the business grew too big for him to do this. In his business life he was scrupulously fair and in his private life somewhat strict: he seldom took a drink having seen some bad effects of alcohol during his early London days. Essentially, he was a man who loved wood and his ability to sense quality was almost uncanny. When he went into business on his own he had one small yard and but a few pounds of capital. When he died the firm had branches in Feltham, Twickenham, Surbiton, Mortlake, Harrow, Hanwell, Worthing and Eastbourne as well as the sawmill and flourishing woodlands at Flimwell. His father (James (1)) had founded a business through his feeling for, and insistence on quality and, on that basis, built it cautiously and carefully. James (2) did likewise with the difference that he was a man of action and imagination – an entrepreneur in fact. It may be wondered what the result might have been if these two remarkable men had stayed together.

It is as well to relate that although James (2) constantly applied himself to his business with the greatest vigour and kept his responsibilities to it always in his mind, he invariably finished his working day at 5.30 pm and devoted his leisure time to his family and to the many forms of sport that he loved. He taught all his children to swim and willingly taught others when on holiday. He played cricket, encouraged his sons to keep a straight bat and was a frequent visitor to the Essex County cricket ground which was then at Leytonstone. As a member of a cycling club he took part in the London to Brighton cycling races that were held in those days. When he moved to Twickenham he became a keen angler, often taking one or other of his sons to Teddington Lock or along the Thames to Shepperton where the sport then was very good. He was also an avid player and follower of billiards and in the Datchet house to which he eventually retired he had a fine billiard room where he found endless pleasure. He taught his sons the game and was proud and gratified when Robert became a County amateur champion.

On the death of James (2) the management of the business was continued in the hands of the four Alsford brothers under the chairmanship of James (3).

Chair used by Her Majesty, The Queen Mother
on her visit to Blundell's School in 1954. It
was made from English oak especially supplied
by Alsfords

The Trade is Freed

A few weeks after the death of James (2) softwood importers were granted freedom to import on their own account timber from the Baltic, the USA and Canada and later in the year softwoods became free from price control although consumer licensing was still maintained. The softwood trade continued its pressure on the government to remove consumer control and in November 1953 consumer licensing was abolished. After 14 years the trade was at last free and Alsfords were once again able to offer their customers what they wanted. Shortly after this, all building restrictions were abolished with the result that the demand for timber sharply increased. The company responded to these events by opening a branch at Cobham in Surrey. The ending of building restrictions also allowed much overdue rebuilding and extensions in the Alsford branches as well as extensive enlargement and development of the Feltham complex which were again carried out under the supervision of William and Arthur Alsford. They were not easy taskmasters for they could judge by eye alone if bricks were not laid correctly: a sloppy bricklayer would be sent away, his work knocked down and rebuilt by a new man or by one of the brothers himself – for they had a principle that they had no right to demand work of others that they could not do themselves.

The years 1957 and 1959 are noteworthy for two important internal innovations that concerned the company's staff. The first of these was the formation of a personnel committee, comprising representatives of all the branches, to promote good relations between staff and employers; to encourage and train all staff and to select suitable employees for promotion. There were also regular meetings to discuss such matters as welfare and wage differentials and the prevention of accidents. This arrangement was found to be invaluable to the running of the business.

Staff Insurance

The step taken in 1959 was one of the most important in the history of the company: this was the starting of Alsfords' own pension scheme. James (3) had attended a meeting of the National Association of Pension Funds and there heard a lecture given by a Mr Andrews, pension and investment manager of Unilever Limited.

Following this James (3) had discussions with a close friend of his, Alfred Harvey of the stockbroking firm of E. J. Collins & Company. These discussions confirmed James' assessment of the immense advantages that would benefit all concerned if the company operated its own pension scheme. At that time 15 Alsford managerial staff were covered by outside policies but it was evident that the new scheme would provide more personal involvement for both firm and staff.

The insurance business has little in common with that of timber, so a great deal of preliminary research and inquiry was necessary before the idea could be implemented and this James carried out with the enthusiastic support of his brothers and senior executives. A number of firms were consulted, including Unilever who were particularly helpful, and with the skilled help of the company's advisers the scheme was finalised and brought into operation on 1st October 1960 under the name of the J. Alsford Limited Pension Scheme.*

The scheme was started with the sum of £40,000 subscribed mainly by James, William and Arthur Alsford in the form of preference and ordinary shares in the company, together with the cash received from the 15 cancelled insurance policies. Through a conservative investment policy followed over the next few years the fund grew to the extent that it became possible to extend the scheme to cover all employees over the age of 25. Today it has 120 members and benefits 24 Alsford pensioners and the value of the fund has risen to £1.5 million. Much of the success of the pension scheme is due to its timely formation and the keen financial discernment of its board of directors.

In 1958 Robert Alsford had resigned from the board of J. Alsford Limited but he subsequently joined the board of J. Alsford Pension Trustees Limited to give the fund the benefit of his special financial knowledge. Details concerning the establishment and operation of the Pension Trust can be found in Appendix 4.

*J. Alsford Limited take this opportunity of thanking the following for their invaluable help and advice in the formation of the scheme:
Bacon & Woodrow; Actuarial Consultants
E. J. Collins & Company; Stockbrokers
Hackett, Radley & Johnson; Accountants
Wilkinson, Kimbers & Staddon; Solicitors

Reorganisation of the Board

In September 1960, far-reaching changes in the board's structure were announced by James (3). He, whilst remaining as chairman, gave up his position as managing director, leaving his brothers William and Arthur as joint managing directors. Three new directors were then appointed – Harry Osborne, Bob D'eath and William John Alsford. Osborne and D'eath were the first board members who were not members of the Alsford family. Harry Osborne joined the firm as a junior salesman in 1933 at the age of 16. Within six years he was made manager of the Mortlake yard and in 1941 was further promoted as manager of the Twickenham branch. Ten years later he moved to Feltham as sales manager to the company and at the time of his appointment to the board he was the firm's commercial manager.

As has been related Bob D'eath started his career with the company in 1933 as a junior clerk with Alsford & Miles Limited and he moved with them to Feltham when the two firms merged in 1939. There he was given the position of cashier and office manager, later progressing to the job of buying softwoods and sundries, working in collaboration with Harry Osborne. The two men made a perfect combination, for Osborne was essentially a practical man with a thorough knowledge of wood, whilst D'eath was a first-class businessman with little or no practical ability. Together they worked as a team and contributed much to the company's post-war expansion.

Feltham Depot, showing Alsfords' method of stacking timber at that time

Two of today's branches. Hanwell . . .

. . . and Eastbourne

Layout for self-service timber

The third new director, John Alsford (the present chairman) is the son of William and great-grandson of James (1). Born in 1934, he attended Blundell's School in 1947–51 and after a year's work in the family firm, qualified as a pilot during his two year's service with the RAF. He re-joined the company in 1954 and spent the next two years gaining knowledge and experience in all sides of the business. He developed a special interest in mechanical handling and production planning and eventually became works and production manager.

The new board made no alterations in the company's general policies or administration, for these were so proven as to need no change; the reconstitution of the board was rather to broaden its outlook so that it would be in a better position to deal with the plans in hand for further expansion and development.

In the event, James (3) only remained as chairman long enough to guide the company into its new programme and when in 1963 this was well under way he resigned his position whilst remaining on the board in an advisory capacity. His place as chairman was taken by his nephew John Alsford who also became joint managing director with Harry Osborne. The board was enlarged in 1966 by the

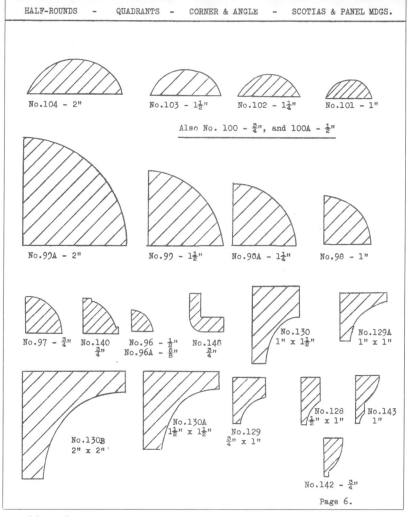

No.104 – 2"   No.103 – 1½"   No.102 – 1¼"   No.101 – 1"

Also No. 100 – ¾", and 100A – ½"

No.99A – 2"   No.99 – 1½"   No.98A – 1¼"   No.98 – 1"

No.97 – ¾"   No.140   No.96 – ½"   No.148   No.130   No.129A
            ¾"   No.96A – ⅜"   ¾"   1" x 1½"   1" x 1"

No.130A   No.128   No.143
1½" x 1½"   ½" x 1"   1"
No.130B
2" x 2"   No.129
            ¾" x 1"

No.142 – ¾"

Page 6.

Mouldings from a 1950 catalogue

appointment as a director of L. H. (George) Halls who had joined the firm in 1941 as a 16-year-old clerk. His career with Alsfords was interrupted by four years service with the RAF but after his return in 1946 his progress was steady. After a series of managerial posts in the branches he was eventually made south-coast regional manager. His position on the board is now south-coast director.

Further Expansion

In line with the firm's traditional policy the expansion programme of the 1960s proceeded steadily and with caution. In 1961 the old-established Hastings timber business of D. J. Neame & Son was purchased and, in 1963, that of W. Key & Son Limited of Berkhamsted. In the following year a sales branch was opened on the Flimwell site. This, being well off the main road and virtually within a wood, was seen as a gamble but it grew slowly and steadily and eventually exceeded all expectations.

Another important development of the 1960s was the introduction of a self-service system to a number of the branches. This move originated in a visit to the USA made by Harry Osborne during which he made a study of 'serve yourself' timber shops already established there. In these, customers browse and pick their requirements from a display of timber and other materials already sorted into types and sizes; accessories are also available. On his return Harry Osborne wrote a series of detailed reports on the system which was studied by the board with the result that self-service was tried at a number of yards. To further develop the idea, another visit to the USA was later made by John Alsford and George Halls.

The advantages of the serve-yourself system were soon apparent. No longer did the customer have to ask for a particular material and size, for he could himself see, feel and test the materials for suitability to his purpose, whether timber, moulding, plywood, chipboard, hardboard, fencing, trellis etc. It was also found that the self-service system particularly suited Alsfords' main customer, the small tradesman, who knows exactly what he wants and requires no sales assistant. No longer did he have to wait impatiently while a housewife described the kind of shelf she intended to put up. Before long there were self-service showrooms at many of the firm's branches – all designed by Harry Osborne. In Britain this was yet another Alsford 'first' which was soon imitated throughout the country.

An internal adjustment worthy of recording occurred in 1965 when, to simplify accounting procedures, J. Alsford Limited bought back all the properties held by the Alsford Land Investment Company Limited which was then wound up.

But by far the most important event of the 1960s was the company's decision to build its own wharf at Rye in Sussex. This was another landmark in the history of Alsfords.

PART 3

The Business Today

As we have seen, since about 1923 most of the firm's imported timber arrived at the Surrey docks to be loaded on to barges, taken up river to wharves in and around Twickenham and transported to the various yards and latterly to the Feltham headquarters. But in 1949 Britain was subjected to a major dock strike which severely interfered with all the functions of the timber trade. Such disruptions became a recurring nuisance involving as they did an ever-present threat of timber being diverted to foreign ports or left sweating in holds of ships held idle for long periods. At the Surrey docks the timber trade found itself more and more subject to the whims and actions of many outside bodies that handle timber – dock labourers, talleymen, stevedores, lightermen and lorry drivers – a strike by any of which brought the others to a standstill. To avoid these troubles and reduce the likelihood of disruption, the firm in the 1950s transferred a proportion of its business to Shoreham docks which, compared with London, were relatively peaceful. Then, as other importers followed this example, difficulties arose there. Public wharves and facilities were stretched to the limit and goods were left unprotected on the quay for long periods. And another difficulty then arose in both Surrey and Shoreham docks.

This was an apparent 'couldn't care less' attitude and a general lack of discipline on the part of dock workers. Before the war they

Unloading timber at Rye Wharf

acted with care, covering the barges or hatches immediately it rained – for otherwise they lost their jobs. But with that threat removed, the general attitude was one of indifference to the cargoes. It is easy to imagine the risks of importing timber under such conditions and the hazards of damage through indifferent handling from ship to barge and from barge to lorry. Therefore, in 1960, the company began considering the possibility of building and operating its own wharf.

The advantages to the firm in having its own wharfing facilities were considerable and can be listed:

1) The whole basis of operations would be secure inasmuch as there would be complete and immediate control plus adequate protection of all goods from shipside to sheds.

2) The direct and regulated delivery of goods from wharf to branches in quantities as and when desired.

3) The avoidance of double or treble handling and the costs involved by imported goods going through Feltham.

Rye Wharf, June 1968 – the first stage of development completed

4) The delivery to Feltham of regulated quantities, in ordered sequence for both the mill and for stock generally.

5) The overall reduction of stock at Feltham and the removal of any need to increase storage facilities there as the firm expanded.

6) A wharf would open up trade throughout a wide area of Surrey and Sussex thus facilitating future anticipated expansion in those counties.

The decision was a difficult one to reach, for there were many weighty matters to be considered, not the least being the large capital investment required. But much of Alsfords' success is due to its ability to assess and adjust to changing conditions and to recognise opportunities when they arise. It did not take long to show that the board's decision to proceed with the scheme was the right one.

Between 1962 and 1963, several possible locations for the wharf were considered and eventually a 12 acre site at Rye Harbour was decided upon and purchased for £12,000.

Building starts

Rye

The ancient town of Rye in Sussex has harboured small ships for hundreds of years. In the 11th century it was a fishing village and during the reign of Henry II it became one of the Cinque Ports. Its importance as a harbour dwindled from the 16th century onwards owing to the steady recession of the tide so that by the time Alsfords arrived the River Rother was but a small estuary with its mouth two miles from the town, but still serving as a harbour, with an average depth of 15 feet at high tide. The only seaborne traffic was occasional small ships carrying coal, grain, timber, stones, and manure. The Alsford site was subject to flooding at high tide and the first operation was to build a retaining wall along the 600 foot frontage to the river – but this could not be started before planning permission was obtained and thus began a long and involved struggle with the East Sussex County Council.

In 1965 there was a planning enquiry which resulted in a decision to deny the company permission to build – and this was in opposition of the declared views of the Rye Borough Council and, for that matter, those of the majority of local residents who realised that the wharf would benefit the town. But there were strong objections from local conservationists and, no doubt, it was their views that persuaded the planning committee to refuse the application.

Alsfords appealed against this decision and to settle the matter an inspector was appointed by the Minister of Housing and Local Government. There can be little doubt that in considering the appeal the inspector was much influenced by a statement made by the Town Clerk of Rye.

> 'When the County Planning Committee's decision to refuse permission was reported to the Town Council...I was instructed to convey the Council's strong protest at this disregard of local opinion...there was the overwhelming support of local residents as indicated at a public meeting. The decision, therefore, makes a mockery of the professed desire of the County Planning Officer to know the feelings of the local people.'

The Rye Harbour Sailing Club was also in favour of the project on the grounds that it would induce the Kent River Authority to improve and maintain the harbour facilities which 'in recent years have been so badly neglected'. In September 1966, the inspector allowed the company's appeal – a decision which was accepted by the Minister. Private enterprise had prevailed over bureaucracy.

Building a Wharf

Although the result of the enquiry was most satisfactory, it had cost the firm a great deal of valuable time, for it left only seven months in which to draw up detailed plans and quantity estimates and to obtain tenders for the work. This was due to the introduction of the Land Development Bill which stipulated that unless the work was put in hand before 5th April 1967, the company would become liable to pay some £80,000 in tax. When received, the tenders ranged from £120,000 to £160,000; the lowest was accepted and building began on 23rd March 1967.

All the operations were put under the direct supervision of John Alsford who was determined that the carefully planned specifications of construction were strictly adhered to and that the work came up to the high standard that was also an Alsford family tradition. Through the specialised knowledge of reinforced concrete techniques which he had learned from his father and uncles John was well qualified for this job. The first stage was the piling of the river bank and the building of the retaining wall. Then the quay was begun – which, because of the soft nature of the ground, involved sinking sheet-steel and case-piles some 45 feet deep. In the meantime, dredging operations were started to allow for the passage of ships with up to 15 foot draught.

An aerial view of the continuing development at Rye Wharf

Rye Wharf berths at full capacity

Work proceeded according to schedule and within a year the wharf was sufficiently complete to receive its first ship. Apart from the speed with which this major piece of engineering was carried out, there was only one incident worth recording. During the levelling of a small hill on the site it was learned that the body of a German pilot had been buried there after his plane crashed during the war. The contractor's men refused to dig on the spot, so John Alsford, watched by a small crowd of workmen and local people, dug deep until he unearthed the bones of the unfortunate airman: these were removed by the police and work continued.

In June 1968 the first timber-sheds were built and the first crane purchased: during the same month the wharf was officially opened with suitable celebrations in the presence of the firm's directors and the local dignitaries. During the festivities, the motor vessel *Dina* arrived at the wharf to unload a cargo of timber and hardboard. Alsfords had brought the largest ship ever up the River Rother. During the remaining six months of 1968, 10 more ships were handled at Rye Wharf bringing in between them 2,000 standards of timber and during the following years the number of vessels using the wharf increased steadily until by 1973 it had reached 130. This rapid increase in traffic was mainly due to the fact that shippers of cargoes other than timber were attracted from the larger ports (such as London) by the advantages of the quick turn-round that Rye offered. It is not unusual, for example, for a 500-ton cargo arriving at

6.00 am to be unloaded on to lorries and on its way to its destination by mid-afternoon on the same day. Another inducement was that harbour dues at Rye were still no more than a shilling (5p) per net registered ton – a rate that had remained unchanged since 1801.

Throughout this period of establishment and growth the construction of the wharf continued until today, after the laying of a total of 43,000 tons of concrete, there are seven cargo sheds with a total floor area of $4\frac{1}{2}$ acres and a full range of modern mechanical handling machinery. Rye Wharf is now the receiving depot for 95 per cent of the company's imported timber which is there subjected to a basic Alsford grading before being sent to Feltham and the firm's various branches. Today the wharf, with its berthing for three vessels, is the basis of a small but busy port. Its staff of 26 deal with 175 ships a year of which about 12 bring in timber. The rest bring talc, fertilisers, chemicals, rubber and various commodities destined for other industries and are reloaded with outgoing cargoes, such as local grain for the continent. The Rye project has proved so successful that plans are in hand for developing the site and its facilities still further. Thus, in establishing a wharf for its own convenience, the firm diversified into wharfing at a time when there was a need and demand for smaller wharfing facilities which are not so liable to be affected by national dock disputes. This was the fourth milestone in the company's history.

General view of the working area at Rye Wharf

Progress at Flimwell

During the early stages of the development of Rye Wharf, it was decided to install a new saw mill at the Flimwell works. The original machinery had served the firm well for 19 years, but it had been somewhat primitive from the start and now, ageing, it was proving incapable of dealing efficiently with the increasing flow of home-grown timber passing through the works. Consequently, the Flimwell manager, Herbert Edwards, together with John Alsford visited a number of sawmills in Europe looking for ideas to include in a design for a new plant. It was eventually settled that the ideal machine for Alsfords' purposes would be one capable of sawing different types of wood into a variety of sizes with the provision for resawing them when required. This posed a problem that seemed at first insurmountable for no such machine had ever been constructed. It would be better and safer, Alsfords were told, to stick to the old method and to employ men to take the sawn planks off one machine and transfer them to another. But the company was determined that the mechanisation it wanted was a practical possibility and, after lengthy research and consultations with sawmill machinery and conveyor-belt manufacturers, a basic machine was adapted that reduces round timber to manageable sizes and dimensions and then resaws them to required sizes: it can deal with logs up to 30 foot long by 4′ 6″ diameter and reduce them, if necessary to 1″ × 1″ pieces – it can also cross-cut to remove faults or ends.

Home-grown timber at Flimwell sawmill

A variety of products stacked for drying

Work on the installation of the new plant began in 1969. A number of firms were involved in the operation under the direct supervision of John Alsford. First, a new, much larger, mill-shed was built over and enclosing the old: the latter was then demolished. Then the new machinery was set up beside the old plant which, when the transfer of work was complete, was dismantled and removed. The work took 12 months, during which production remained uninterrupted in spite of the large number of earth-movers, builders and engineers who were working over the entire production area. When operations were complete, the new mill came up to all expectations and now cuts over 100,000 cubic feet of timber a year.

Started as an expedient on a site that was little more than a wooded quagmire, the plant at Flimwell is today acknowledged as one of the most efficient of its kind in the country. It is not only an instance of the Alsford touch, but an example to British industry of what can be done, given the need and the resolution to satisfy it.

Years of Change

In February 1969, James, William and Arthur Alsford gave up their directorships and retired from the company with a combined service between them of 153 years. This left John as the only Alsford remaining on the board. The steady and sustained growth of the company since the end of World War 2 was due to the joint efforts and unanimity of opinion of the four third-generation Alsfords, and it is said that in all their years of directing the company there was never a need for a vote to be taken at a board meeting. This was due to the fact that they all held to the simple policy of their father and grandfather – to expand by opening branches with finance generated by the firm's profits – which meant squeezing assets out of the business by dint of hard work and shrewd judgement: they also stuck to the family tradition of never resting on their laurels.

On their retirement, it must have been with some satisfaction that they contemplated the results of the family's labours since the firm moved to Heath Road in 1914. From a small yard with a dilapidated shed it had evolved to become a large organisation employing over 220 people, with mills, 11 thriving branches, its own woodlands and a busy wharf handling scores of ships a year. They had seen many changes in the timber industry since those early days – timber-packaging (which arrived in Britain in the mid-'50s); truck-bundling, pre-slinging and even the wrapping of wood had become standard terms in the timber trade's vocabulary. The timber-porter with his leather shoulder-pad had gone and the firm's horse-drawn carts and early motor-vans had been replaced by a fleet of 25 vans and lorries ranging in weight from 3 to 32 tons.

Present head office building at Feltham

Arthur, Bill, James (3) and Bob Alsford c1968

Interlude – Heap Strange Object

In the Alsford branch at Berkhamsted stands a 27 foot-high Indian totem pole which was erected by the company in 1970. Several of the branches in south-east England had been recently developed and a considerable amount of Canadian red cedar had been used for outside cladding and, as totem-poles are usually carved from a single cedar log, John Alsford considered that it would be a novel idea to obtain a specimen for one of the branches. Enquiries were made in British Columbia and with the co-operation of a British Columbian museum, the company commissioned Henry Hunt, a Kwakiutl Indian from Vancouver Island to carve a totem-pole. A special 3-ton cedar log was selected and the pole carved and sent to England. It was erected at Berkhamsted in June 1970, where it still attracts visitors from miles around.

Alsfords in the 1970s

There were further developments in the opening years of the 1970s with the introduction of self-service facilities in some branches and the starting of a new yard in 1972 at Uckfield. In 1971, Alfred Smith, the company secretary, joined the board of directors.   Having

85

Chief carver, Henry Hunt with his assistant Tony Hunt, carving the
totem-pole in Thunderbird Park, Victoria BC
PROVINCIAL MUSEUM, VICTORIA BC

RIGHT Totem-pole standing by the Grand Union canal at Berkhamsted
GAZETTE, HEMEL HEMPSTEAD

started as a ledger-clerk in 1948, Alfred Smith was later appointed
personal secretary to James, William and Arthur Alsford – an
exacting job which taught him a great deal of company procedure.
As a result he was made secretary to the company in 1963 and
qualified as a chartered secretary in 1968. There were further
additions to the board in 1973 when Robert Alsford rejoined as
economic adviser. Also appointed was James Howes, son of Winifred
Howes, the elder daughter of James (2). In 1930 she had married
Kenneth Howes who started a builders' and timber merchant
business in Hounslow (where it still exists) and when James Howes
completed his military service in 1952, he took a job as a salesman at
Alsfords' Twickenham yard. After working his way through various
departments he was made stock-controller. Another newcomer to
the board at this time was Rodney Osborne, the son of Harry
Osborne. He had spent many years with the company training in
accountancy. He left for a short while to further his experience and
re-joined as an accountant in 1970.

During the first half of the 1970s, Alsfords were for the most part
occupied in consolidating the considerable progress that had been

achieved during the previous 10 years particularly in the completion
and further improvement of the Rye complex. Then, in 1976, further
expansion of the firm's ownership of woodlands was made through
the purchase of a 450-acre forest at Goudhurst in Kent, in which
stood a fine mixture of trees in various stages of maturity. This
brought the company's ownership of woodlands to over 500 acres
and, as a long term project, it was an important step towards
ensuring future supplies of home-grown timber for Flimwell.

The year 1977 was a sad one for the company, for in January
occurred the death of the third James Alsford at the age of 76. In life
he was a man of unusual energy and self-confidence with an
insatiable interest in all aspects of the timber trade. An active
cricketer in his early years he retained a love of the game throughout

The West German coaster *Thekla* stranded on the river Rother in February
1975. On her way to unload at Rye Wharf she struck the harbour wall,
ran aground and disrupted traffic for a week

his life. In his latter years he became a keen sailing enthusiast and
this newly-found love of the sea led his interest to the training of
young people. At the end of 1973 he and his wife Doris set up a new
charitable trust and made over to it a substantial holding of shares in
the company. Since its inception this trust, known as the Alsford
Charitable Trust, has given and continues to give financial help to
many deserving causes and in particular those associated with
young people such as the Sail Training Association. James' absolute
integrity, wide experience and sound judgement commanded respect
from all with whom he came into contact and he was sadly missed,
not only by the Alsford family but by all who knew him throughout
his long business life. A visible reminder of his efforts for the company
is the Alsford registered trade mark which he designed in 1953.

The company suffered another loss in 1978 when Bob D'eath died
suddenly in September. He had retired from full-time work only six
months before and at the time of his death was still working part time
in his old department. During his 45 years of continuous service he
contributed much to the firm's success.

Another first class sales outlet was secured in 1978 by the
purchase of Rye's only timber merchants, Thomas Hinds & Sons

(Rye) Limited. This busy concern blended well with Alsfords' wharfing facilities and obviated the firm's intention of opening a branch on or near the wharf itself.

Another timber business was purchased in 1978. This was none other than the Colchester firm of J. Alcoe (Colchester) Limited, a branch of the company that had sprung from the Manor Park timber yard which James (1) had given to his daughter Louisa on her marriage to John Alcoe. The latter's son, Edward Alcoe, considerably enlarged that business and opened the Colchester branch in 1960. At the time of its purchase by Alsfords it was under the management of Edward's son, Keith, who had in fact served a year's apprenticeship with Alsfords before joining his family's business. Thus, after more than a century, the link between the Alsford and Alcoe families was renewed.

In 1979 the board was augmented by the appointment as a director of David Edwards, manager at Flimwell and son of Herbert Edwards who had discovered the site and managed it for 23 years before he retired in 1974. In the same year, Arthur Alsford accepted an invitation to rejoin the board as a director and deputy chairman, thus strengthening it with his long experience of all aspects of the timber trade.

The Company Today

J. Alsford Limited now operates on an extensive and diverse scale, with a staff of almost 300 people supplying timber and many other building requirements from 16 outlets spread over Britain's most populous and prosperous region. Its wharf handles virtually all the directly imported softwoods and these are supplemented by nearly 2,000 cubic metres of hard and softwood produced by its own 500 acres and surrounding woodlands. All this evolved from the small yard established at Leyton by the first James Alsford a hundred years ago. This growth, which has been continuous and deliberate, is marked by four milestones in the company's history. The move to Twickenham to take advantage of the building boom that was taking place in that area: the development of the Feltham depot and the merging of the importing and retailing sides of the business at a most opportune time; the diversification into the home-grown timber trade at a moment when there was a considerable demand for native

The board: from left David Edwards, Jimmy Howes, Rodney Osborne, Bob Alsford, Alfred Smith, John Alsford, Harry Osborne, Arthur Alsford and George Halls

wood and the bold decision to build a wharf at Rye to counter the rise of industrial disputes in dockland and to make the firm largely self-sufficient. All these developments demonstrate the company's inherited ability of being able to evaluate economic and industrial trends and to adjust to and take advantage of them.

Two other important factors have contributed to Alsfords' success. First, the recognition of the importance of good staff-management relations, for in dealing with its employees the company is known for its forward and progressive outlook. This is particularly remarkable in the matter of teaching its traditional skills to the younger staff-members. In this respect, the aim is to give each youth with the necessary aptitude and capability a thorough training inside the mills and the opportunity for technical study outside: this is to enable him, if he works hard and takes advantage of these opportunities, to take his place in the timber industry as a technician or a craftsman who will reflect credit not only on himself but on the company who trained him. One of the results of this policy is that the firm is usually able to promote staff from within and most of its executives are people who have worked their way up in the firm – usually from the yards. Thus it follows that the strength of the present board is due to the fact that all its members are practical, working men in their particular sphere of operation, each capable of standing-in at times of crisis. Staff do seem to stay with Alsfords – a fact that is demonstrated by the list of long-serving members which is printed in Appendix 2.

The second factor is that the company has had the advantage of the dedicated and continuous efforts of one family through four generations, all possessing a respect for and understanding of wood – and in particular the members of the last three, each of whom has had drummed into him the policy that high quality should over-ride every other consideration. In this way, Alsfords reflect the traditional virtues so often associated with a family business – that of caring about their customers, caring for and proud of their reputation and, above all, caring about the goods they sell.

Here ends the story of the first hundred years of Alsfords. It is a record of steady progress which reflects credit not only on those who founded and built the business but on the workings of the private enterprise system that made it possible. What the future holds for the company cannot be foretold for there will, no doubt, be difficulties to meet, problems to be solved and risks to be run – just as there were throughout the firm's long past. But, by cautiously and firmly following the precepts upon which the company was founded and subsequently grew, and by keeping its assets in a condition to meet all emergencies while yet allowing for further growth, the present directors are ensuring that the story of Alsfords is far from finished. Thus, it faces the future with confidence.

The Future

by W. John Alsford

SINCE THE BEGINNING OF TIME the world has been, and still is, undergoing constant change. This has also been so with J. Alsford Limited over the past one hundred years, as is evident after reading the history of the company and changes will, undoubtedly, continue as we advance into our next century of trading.

But there are things I would loathe to see change; one being that which has enabled our company to survive and prosper during its first one hundred years of trading in the face of competition, and for which we are primarily known . . .

'Alsfords for Quality Timber'.

Not only are we renowned for 'Quality Timber', but also for the things associated with it. For example – 'tidiness' and 'good housekeeping'; two virtues we endeavour to instil into our employees, and for which (it is reputed) makes us one of the tidiest timber importers and timber merchants in the United Kingdom, or even in Western Europe.

This emphasis on 'quality' means that quality management is also required, because without this prerequisite, policies and decisions cannot be implemented.

Giving a better service than your competitor is what being a prosperous company is all about!

Now in 1982, we do not think that we have a divine right to retain customers, who we have had the pleasure to serve, unless we give them the quality of service they require and deserve. This way, we can not only enjoy a major reputation based on our past record, but we can also look forward to the future and our next one hundred years with confidence.

I believe there is no reason why we should not continue to be one of the country's leading family-owned private companies provided we can resist the temptation and pressures of take-over offers or, indeed, find ourselves having to sell shares publicly because of taxation. I hope that I can continue the practice of my forebears and train my own son, James, to the same standards that are a tradition in the Alsford family, and thus keep our lineage for at least the best part of another century.

My fervent hope is that the spirit of co-operation and goodwill that has been engendered between management and staff will long continue, because without it our company would fail. Indeed, our policy must not change from the utmost care and attention that we give to this important aspect of our success, and with the now very soundly-established Pension Company, there is no reason why our employees should not enjoy the benefits that accrue to them by the time of their retirement.

The company may have grown slowly in the eyes of some critics, but I like to recall something I once read:

> 'Let me look upward toward
> the branches of a towering oak
> And remember that it grew great
> and strong because it grew slowly'

It is the soundness of our growth that means so much.

I believe there is scope for us to expand not only within the area in which we now operate, namely the south-eastern part of the United Kingdom but (with the advent of faster air travel making the world markets smaller) we may wish to seek still farther horizons in other parts of this diminishing world; especially those lands which would welcome our expertise in providing service and quality which we know is required by those customers who appreciate the care and attention we give to every piece of timber handled.

Finally, I must express my thanks to Patrick Bowen of Henry Melland Limited for suggesting in a persuasive manner that this history should be written, and for introducing the author – Patrick Beaver – to our company and members of the Alsford family.

It is Patrick Beaver who has managed to piece together the complexities of our past, and has written a most interesting book not only for the company, employees and the Alsford family but, hopefully, to a much wider circle of friends who will find it as fascinating to read as have those members of the family and company who have helped in its preparation to enable its publication in this our Centenary Year.

Appendix 1

Chronological summary of the History of J. Alsford Limited

1808   James Alsford, cabinet-maker, born
1841   James Alsford (1) born
1871   James (1) emigrates to Canada
1874   James (1) returns to England, marries and starts firewood business at Wood Green
1877   James (1) starts timber yard at Edmonton
1878   James (2) born
1882   *Leyton business started and the Alsford Tradition commences*
1892   James (2) starts work in the business
1893   James (1) loses hand in sawmill accident
1898   Disagreement between James (1) and James (2)
1899   James (2) marries Elizabeth Cullingworth
1901   James (3) born
1903   William Alsford born
1905   Arthur Alsford born
1908   James (1) retires from business
1908   Winifred Alsford born
1910   May Alsford born
1912   Death of James (1)
1914   Business moved to 52 Heath Road, Twickenham
1914   Robert Alsford born
1916   James (2) joins Army and James (3) takes over the management of the business
1917   William Alsford joins the business
1919   James (2) returns to business
1921   Arthur Alsford enters the business
1921   63/65 Heath Road, Twickenham purchased and the business expanded

1922	Mortlake branch opened
1922	Barging started to Twickenham
1924	67/69 Heath Road, Twickenham purchased
1926	Surbiton branch started
1926	Winifred Alsford enters the business
1928	'Do-it-Yourself' shop opened at Twickenham
1929	Robert Alsford enters the business
1932	Alsford & Miles Limited founded
1932	Raynes Park branch opened
1933	James (2) retires
1933	H. R. Osborne and W. R. J. D'eath join the Company
1934	W. John Alsford (the present Chairman) born
1936	Hanwell branch purchased
1937	Feltham site purchased
1938	Alsford Land Investment Company Limited founded
1939	South Harrow branch started
1939	J. Alsford merges with Alsford & Miles Limited and the name is changed to J. Alsford Limited
1939	Leyton yard closed
1943	Worthing branch acquired
1946	Felling at Wadhurst started and sawmill erected there
1946	Eastbourne branch purchased
1949	Yellowcoat Wood, Flimwell purchased and sawmill set up
1950	Planting started at Flimwell
1951	Death of James (2)
1953	Cobham branch opened
1960	J. Alsford Limited Pension Scheme founded
1960	Reorganisation of the Board of Directors and the appointment of the first non-family directors
1961	Hastings branch purchased
1963	Berkhamsted branch purchased
1963	Site for wharf purchased at Rye
1965	Alsford Land Investment Company Limited wound up
1967	Building started at Rye
1968	Rye Wharf in operation
1969	James, William and Arthur Alsford retire from the Board
1970	New plant installed at Flimwell
1970	Totem-pole erected at Berkhamsted
1972	Uckfield branch opened
1976	Woodlands at Goudhurst purchased
1977	Death of James (3)
1978	Rye branch purchased
1978	Colchester branch purchased
1979	Arthur Alsford rejoins the Board
1982	J. Alsford Limited Centenary Year

Appendix 2

Present J. Alsford Limited employees with over 21 years' service to the end of 1981

		Years' Service
H. R. Osborne	Joint Managing Director	48
R. C. Hunt	Branch Manager	45
C. Howells	Branch Manager	42
L. H. Halls	South Coast Director	40
L. G. E. Saunders	Sales Supervisor	40
H. Burgess	Service Mill Supervisor	38
H. J. Pooley	Saw Doctor	35
R. L. Davies	Relief Branch Manager	35
H. J. Edwards	Forestry Adviser	35
D. A. McRae-Adams	Driver	34
D. C. Barrow	Sawyer	34
G. Dengate	Driver	34
L. C. Neville, FIM(Wood)T, AIIM	Works Manager	33
G. H. Weaver	Yard Assistant	33
R. C. Gardner	Despatch Manager	33
J. G. Hide	Maintenance Supervisor	33
A. G. M. Smith, FCIS	Company Secretary and Director	33
R. G. Hylands	Machinist	31
F. C. Cooley	Driver	30
W. J. Alsford	Chairman and Managing Director	30
K. Colbran	Sales Supervisor	29
E. J. Mepham	Branch Manager	29
J. R. Howes, AIIM	Purchasing Director	29
Mrs T. Clark	Cashier/Clerk	28
R. P. E. Rourke	Tug Driver	27
J. R. Floyd	Assistant to Director	26
R. C. Pankhurst	Machinist	25
A. C. T. Young	Saw Doctor	24
C. D. Bett	Assistant to Purchasing Director	24
W. Hutton	Despatch Assistant	22
K. G. Harris	Yard Assistant	22
D. J. Wright	Yard Assistant	22
E. M. Harris	Fork Lift Driver/Yard Assistant	22
Mrs M. Berryman	Canteen Assistant	22
C. A. Foster	Sawyer	21
C. W. Bennett	Maintenance Assistant	21

In addition to the above, there are a further 36 employees who have each completed 10 years' service

Past employees with over 21 years' service

		Years' Service
J. Alsford (3)	Director	54
W. A. Alsford	Director	52
A. L. Alsford	Director	49
W. R. J. D'eath	Purchasing Director	45
F. A. Wilkie	Saw Doctor	39
J. E. Rhoades-Brown	Sales Supervisor	37
T. M. Rokins	Sales Assistant	34
H. Jacob	Timber Imports/Fork Lift Driver	34
D. W. Angus	Branch Manager	32
L. V. Hollobone	Driver	32
W. Hood	Branch Manager	32
H. Samuels	Mill & Yard Assistant	31
G. R. Grant	Timber Grader	30
E. C. Harrison	Yard Assistant	30
A. H. Manser	Sales Supervisor	30
R. F. Alsford	Director	29
G. E. Catchpole	Kiln Operator	29
W. J. Potter	Sawyer	28
T. A. Leverett	Branch Manager	28
G. F. G. Avenell	Sales Clerk	26
G. S. Duncan	Sawmill Supervisor	26
H. J. Mepham	Branch Manager	25
E. J. Knight	Driver	24
E. H. Cornwill	Branch Manager	24
F. A. Harwood	Branch Supervisor	23
A. S. Fretton	Branch Manager	22
D. W. Green	Yard & Mill Assistant	22
D. D. Ross	Planing Mill Supervisor	22
Miss D. M. Watling	Cashier/Clerk	22
Mrs J. N. F. Palmer	Wages Clerk	21
A. W. Cullingworth	Saw Doctor	21

Appendix 3

List of Establishments

Head Office	Twickenham Road, Hanworth, Feltham, Middlesex TW13 6JJ	Telephone 01-894 1011
Sales Outlets		
Feltham	Twickenham Road, Hanworth	01-894 1011
Twickenham	63/69 Heath Road	01-892 2868
Surbiton	St Mark's Hill	01-399 4234
Mortlake	14 Sheen Lane	01-876 2257
Cobham	61 Portsmouth Road	Cobham 3468
Hanwell	54-62 Uxbridge Road	01-567 0563
South Harrow	Belmont Parade, Northolt Road	01-422 3930
Berkhamsted	Castle Street	Berkhamsted 5325
Eastbourne	Mountfield Road, Hampden Park	Eastbourne 52255
Worthing	King Street	Worthing 200154
Hastings	Chatham Road, Silverhill	Hastings 420101
Flimwell	Yellowcoat Wood Sawmills	Flimwell 368
Uckfield	Bell Lane	Uckfield 2856
Rye	The Strand	Rye 2397
Colchester	24 East Hill	Colchester 866785
Wharf		
Rye	Rye Wharf, Rye Harbour	Rye 2501
Forestry		
Flimwell	Yellowcoat Wood Sawmills	Flimwell 368

Appendix 4

Outline of lecture given by James Alsford (3) to Managers and Executives regarding the J. Alsford Limited Pension Scheme – 18th November, 1964

Address of Welcome to Managers and Executives

I welcome this opportunity of addressing you in regard to the Pension Scheme, which is likely to be my last as I am within a year of my retirement from active service.

Few, if any, in our company are fully aware of the outstanding benefits this Pension Scheme is gradually securing, or appreciate the voluntary services that are so freely being given in building a financially secure future for all concerned.

I earnestly desire, in no uncertain manner, to get over to you all as responsible managers and executives, the full implications of this Pension Scheme so that you will be fully conversant with the Scheme and competent to convey these implications to those employees for whom you are, or will be, responsible.

Brief History of the Pension Scheme and its introduction four years ago

Insurance Companies rarely give more than 3 per cent compound interest and it is often less. Our old Assurance Scheme gave only $2\frac{3}{4}$ per cent.

The Assurance Scheme allowed only 120ths of salary for each year of service as against our improved conditions.

Although the Assurance Scheme only commenced in 1948, we went back to the commencement in service of every employee joining the company and paid all the contributions to finance the past service.

Members contributions as a percentage of salary under the Assurance Scheme was 10 per cent. Under the J. Alsford Limited Pension Scheme it is now considerably less.

The old scheme ignored any alterations in salary over the last five years of service and was therefore based on salary at 60 years of age. The J. Alsford Limited Pension Scheme provides for pensions to be calculated on the best three consecutive years in the last 10 years of service.

Relief from Income Tax under the Assurance Scheme was allowed only in respect of Life Assurance premiums but the contributions to the J. Alsford Limited Pension Scheme are allowed in full as a deduction for Income Tax purposes

The J. Alsford Limited Pension Scheme
Security and Control

In the first place, a Pension Scheme had to be submitted to and approved by the Inland Revenue.

Annual Accounts must be submitted to the Inland Revenue.

Actuarial assessments of liabilities and assets are required to be made every five years or more frequently if considered necessary by the Trustees.

Income or capital is not allowed by the Inland Revenue to become excessive or grossly out of proportion to its liabilities.

Tax Advantages

All Members contributions are allowed in full as a deduction for Income Tax.

Pension Fund – The total revenue is free from Income or Profits Taxes.

Interest Earned

From the value for money point of view, which means the money of both employers and employees, a private scheme such as ours will always come out on top as money paid into it earns interest whereas contributions to any state scheme do not.

Finally

We brought into our own pension scheme every employee of every grade, whereas before entry was limited mainly to managers and executives.

The cost of all this, with its consequent advantage to all employees, was funded at the commencement by the Company which made a gift of about £25,000.

The J. Alsford Limited Pension Scheme commenced in October 1960 and has now been in being for about four years.

Recommendation and Advice of Mr Andrews, Pension and Investment Manager of Unilever Limited

The principal purpose of pension funds is to produce income and not capital gains, although that is of course desirable.

The widest possible variety of shares should be purchased but not in your own or any directly connected industry.

Equity shares are a must in investing for pension funds because growth of capital and income is a necessary essential to combat inflation.

Insurance Companies have invested at 50 per cent in equity shares and many do at a much higher ratio.

One of the greatest advantages from any private pension fund is that reserves of capital and income are gradually built up so gratuitous payments are possible to employees to meet any inflationary circumstances during members' retirement.